11-11

The
New
Father

A Dad's Guide
to the First Year

The
New
Father

A Dad's Guide
to the First Year

Armin A. Brott

Abbeville Press • Publishers
New York • London

To Tirzah and Talya,
without whom being a dad just wouldn't be the same

EDITOR: Jacqueline Decter
DESIGNER: Celia Fuller
PRODUCTION EDITOR: Leslie Bockol
PRODUCTION MANAGER: Lou Bilka

First edition
10 9 8 7 6

Cover photograph by Milton Heiberg. For cartoon credits, see page 239.

The Library of Congress has cataloged the paperback edition as follows:
Brott, Armin A.
    The new father : a dad's guide to the first year / Armin A. Brott.
      p.   cm.
    Includes bibliographical references and index.
    ISBN 0-7892-0275-1
    1. Infants.   2. Infants—Care.   3. Father and infant.   I. Title.
HQ774.B777   1997
649'.122—dc21   96-47489

Hardcover edition ISBN 0-7892-0418-5

Contents

Acknowledgments

I'd like to thank the following people (in alphabetical order), whose help has made this book far better—and far more accurate—than it otherwise might have been:

Jim Cameron and the folks at Temperament Talk, whose work on temperament changed my life; Phil and Carolyn Cowan and Ross Parke for their comments, suggestions, and inspiration; Jackie Decter, for her wisdom, insight, patience, sense of humor, and, above all, her sharp eye; Bruce Drobeck, Bruce Linton, and Glen Palm, who, completely independently of each other, have made major contributions to the literature on fatherhood and freely shared their research with me; Celia Fuller, for making me look good with yet another inspired design; Ken Guilmartin and Edward Gordon for their distinct but equally valuable contributions to the sections on music; Amy Handy, for her constructive criticism and for smoothing out the rough edges; Seth Himmelhoch, who more than once magically pulled out from his files precisely what I needed; Pam Jordan, for her wisdom, guts, and encouragement; Jim Levine, for getting everyone together with a minimum of bloodshed; the wonderful, compassionate, and completely selfless folks at the SIDS Alliance; Dawn Swanson, the incredible children's librarian at the Berkeley Public Library, for helping me select—and arrange developmentally—the best kids' books; Eric Tyson, for reviewing, commenting on, and adding to the sections on money and insurance; and finally, Andrea, who put our disagreements aside for the greater good and once again read every word; and my parents, for their hospitality, careful editing, and for not getting too upset when I griped about their parenting techniques—thirty years too late for them to do anything about it.

Introduction

Nobody really knows how or when it started, but one of the most widespread—and most cherished—myths about childrearing is that women are naturally more nurturing than men, that they are instinctively better at the parenting thing, and that men are nearly incompetent.

The facts, however, tell a very different story. A significant amount of research has proven that men are inherently just as nurturing and responsive to their children's needs as women. What too many men (and women) don't realize is that to the extent that women are "better" parents, it's simply because they've had more practice. In fact, the single most important factor in determining the depth of long-term father-child relationships is opportunity. Basically, it comes down to this: "Having children makes you no more a parent than having a piano makes you a pianist," writes author Michael Levine in *Lessons at the Halfway Point*.

"In almost all of their interactions with children, fathers do things a little differently from mothers," writes researcher David Popenoe. "What fathers do—their special parenting style—is not only highly complementary to what mothers do, but by all indications important in its own right for optimum childrearing."

Not surprisingly, then, fathers have very different needs from mothers when it comes to parenting information and resources. But nearly every book, video, seminar, and magazine article on raising kids has been geared specifically to women and to helping them acquire the skills they need to be better parents. Fathers have been essentially ignored—until now.

How This Book Is Different

Because babies develop so quickly, most books aimed at parents of infants (babies from birth through twelve months) are broken down by month. The same goes here. But while the majority of parenting books focus on how babies develop during this period, the primary focus of *The New Father: A Dad's Guide to the First Year* is on how *fathers* develop. This is an approach that has rarely, if ever, been tried. Each of the chapters is divided into three major sections:

What's Going On with the Baby

This section is designed to give you an overview of the four major areas of your baby's development: physical, intellectual, verbal, and emotional/social. A lot of what a man experiences as a father is directly related to, or in response to, his children. So knowing the basics of their growth will help put your own growth into better perspective. Please remember, however, that all babies develop at different rates and that the range of "normal" behavior is very wide. If your baby isn't doing the things covered in the predicted month, don't worry. But if he is six months behind, check with your pediatrician.

What You're Going Through

Because the experience of fatherhood has largely been ignored in parenting books, many men think the feelings they are having are abnormal. In this section we examine at length what new fathers go through and the ways they grow and develop—emotionally and psychologically—over the course of their fatherhood. You're a lot more normal than you think.

You and Your Baby

This section gives you all the tools you need to understand and create the deepest, closest possible relationship with your child—even if you have only half an hour a day to spend with her. In this section we cover topics as diverse as play, music, reading, discipline, and temperament.

Family Matters

A number of the chapters feature a "Family Matters" section in which we discuss a variety of issues that will have a major impact not only on you but also on your family as a whole. Topics include dealing with crying, postpartum depression (which men get too!), childproofing, family finances, and finding appropriate child care.

Why Get Involved?

First, because it's good for your kids. "Everything we know shows that when men are involved with their children, the children's IQ increases by the time they are six or seven," says pediatrician T. Berry Brazelton. Brazelton adds that with the father's involvement "the child is also more likely to have a sense of humor, to develop a sort of inner excitement, to believe in himself or herself, to be more motivated to learn."

In contrast, a father's emotional distance can have a profound negative impact. "Research clearly documents the direct correlation between father absence and higher rates of aggressive behavior in sons, sexually precocious behavior in daughters and more rigid sex stereotypes in children of both sexes," writes Dr. Louise B. Silverstein of New York University.

Second, it's good for you. A mountain of research has shown that fathers who are actively involved with their children are more likely to be happily married and are more likely to advance in their careers. "Being a father can change the ways that men think about themselves," writes Ross Parke, one of the major fatherhood researchers. "Fathering often helps men to clarify their values and to set priorities. It may enhance their self-esteem if they manage its demands and responsibilities well, or alternatively, it may be unsettling and depressing by revealing their limitations and weaknesses. Fathers can learn from their children and be matured by them."

Third, being an involved father is good for your partner and for your marriage. Division of labor issues are the number one marital stressor, and the more support mothers get from their husbands, the happier they are in their marriages and the better they perform their parenting duties. Men whose partners are happy in their marriages tend to be happier themselves. And men who are happy in their marriages are generally more involved in their fathering role. It just never ends; and there's no reason why it should.

A Note on Terminology

He, She, It

In the not so distant past (the present, too, really) parenting books, in which the parent is assumed to be the mother, almost always referred to the baby as "he." While there's an argument to be made that in English the male pronoun is sort of a generic term, I'm pretty sensitive to issues of gender neutrality. And as the father of two girls, I wanted to see at least an occasional "she," just to let me know that what was being said might actually apply to my children. But as a writer, I find that phrases like "his or her," "he or she," and especially "s/he" make for cumbersome reading and awkward sentences. The solution? I decided simply to alternate between "he" and "she" as often as possible. Except in a few specific cases (circumcision, for example), the terms are interchangeable.

Your Partner in Parenting

In the same way that calling all babies "he" discounts the experience of all the "shes" out there, calling all mothers "wives" essentially denies the existence of the many, many other women who have children: girlfriends, lovers, live-in companions, fiancées, and so on. So, to keep from making any kind of statement about the importance (or lack of importance, depending on how you feel) of marriage, I refer to the mother of your child as your "partner," as we did in *The Expectant Father: Facts, Tips, and Advice for Dads-to-Be.*

If Some of This Sounds a Little Familiar . . .

If you read *The Expectant Father* (and if you didn't, it's not too late), you may notice that there's some overlap between the end of that book and the early part of this book. I assure you that this repetition of material is less the result of laziness on my part than of the necessity born of having to cover several of the same important topics in both books.

What This Book Isn't

While there's no doubt that this book is filled with information you can't get anywhere else, it is not intended to take the place of your pediatrician, financial planner, or lawyer. Naturally, I wouldn't suggest that you do anything I wouldn't do (or haven't done already). Still, before blindly following my advice, please check with an appropriate professional.

Coming Home

What's Going On with the Baby

Physically

♦ Although most of your newborn's physical capabilities are run by a series of reflexes (see pages 38–43), she does have some control over her tiny body.

♦ She can focus her eyes—for a few seconds, at least—on an object held 8 to 10 inches from her face, and she may be able to move her head from side to side.

♦ She probably won't eat much for the first 24 hours, but after that, she'll want 7 to 8 feedings each day.

♦ She seems to be doing everything at an accelerated pace: at 33 breaths and 120 heartbeats/minute, her metabolism is moving about twice as fast as yours.

♦ Her intestines are moving even faster: she'll urinate as many as 18 times and move those brand-new bowels 4 to 7 times every 24 hours.

♦ Needing to recover from all that activity, it's no surprise that she spends 80 percent of her time asleep, taking as many as 7 to 8 naps a day.

Intellectually

♦ Right from birth, your baby is capable of making a number of intellectual decisions.

♦ If she hears a sound, she can tell whether it's coming from the right, left, or straight ahead.

♦ She can distinguish between sweet and sour (preferring sweet, like most of us).

♦ She also has a highly developed sense of smell. At seven days, she'll be able to tell the difference between a pad sprinkled with her own mother's milk and one from another mother.

♦ She prefers simple patterns to complex ones and the borders of objects (such as your jaw or hairline) to the inner details (mouth and nose).

♦ She can't, however, differentiate herself from the other objects in her world. When she grasps your hand, for example, her little brain doesn't know whether she's holding her own hand or yours.

Verbally

♦ At this point, most of the vocal sounds your baby produces will be cries or animal-like grunts and squeaks.

Emotionally/Socially

♦ Although she's alert and comfortable for only 30 or so minutes out of every 4 hours, your baby is already trying to make contact with you.

♦ When she hears a voice or other noise, she'll become quiet and try to focus.

♦ She's capable of showing excitement and distress, and will probably be quiet when you pick her up.

What You're Going Through

Comparing How You Imagined the Birth Would Go with How It Went

Let's face it: every expecting couple secretly (or not so secretly) hopes for a pain-free, twenty-minute labor, and nobody ever really plans for a horrible birth experience. Even in childbirth education classes, if the instructor talks at all about the unpleasant things that can happen, she usually refers to them as "contingencies"—a word that makes it seem as though everything is still under control.

If your partner's labor and delivery went according to plan, chances are you're delighted with the way things turned out and you're oohing and ahhing over your baby. But if there were any problems—induced labor, an emergency C-section, a threat to your partner's or your baby's life—your whole impression of the birth process may have changed. It's not unusual in these cases to blame the baby for causing your partner so much physical pain and you so much psychological agony. It can happen easily, without your really being aware of it.

So pay close attention during the first few weeks to how you're feeling about your baby. And if you find yourself being angry or resentful of her, or thinking or saying things—even in jest—such as "All the pain is the baby's fault," or (as I did) "The baby had jammed herself in there sideways and refused to come out," try to remember that no matter how brilliant and talented you think your baby is, she was a completely passive player in the entire process. Giving in to the temptation to blame your baby for *anything* at this point can seriously interfere with your future relationship together.

The Brief "Is This Really My Baby?" Phase

The first thing I did after both my daughters were born was make sure they had two arms and legs, and ten fingers and toes. Once all limbs and extremities were accounted for, I quickly looked over both my daughters to see whether they had "my" nose or chin.

Later on, I felt a little guilty about that—after all, shouldn't I have been hugging and kissing my daughters instead of giving them a full-body inspection? Maybe, but as it turns out, that's what almost all new fathers do within the first few minutes after the birth of their babies. "They immediately look for physical similarities to validate that the child was theirs," says researcher Pamela Jordan. And this happens for a reason: for almost all new fathers—regardless of how many of their partner's prenatal doctor appointments they went to, how many times they heard the baby's heartbeat or saw him squirm around on an ultrasound, and how many times they felt him kick—the baby isn't "real" until *after* the birth, when father and baby have a chance to meet each other face to face. "Seeing the infant emerge from his mate's body through vaginal or cesarean birth is a powerful experience for each father," writes Jordan. "Birth proved that this infant had been the growth within the mother's abdomen."

As it turns out, only one of my daughters has "my" chin, and it's looking like both of them will go through life without my nose (and, hopefully, the accompanying sinus problems). But what I really found disheartening at the time was that neither of them shared the Brott family webbed toes (it isn't all that noticeable, but it helps my swimming immeasurably).

Babies hardly ever look exactly as you imagined they would before they were born. And being disappointed about a nose, a chin, or even some toes is something you'll get over soon enough—especially when you discover in a few weeks that the baby does have something of yours (they always do).

But what if the baby has a penis or a vagina when you were expecting the opposite? Getting a boy when you expected a girl, or vice versa, can be a real shock. "When one's fantasy is not fulfilled, there is a period of regret for what might have been," writes Ellen Galinsky, head of the Work and Family Institute. "And this unhappiness can stand in the way of the parents' reaching out, accepting the baby."

Fortunately, things don't have to be this way. The conflict between fantasy and reality, says Galinsky, "can also be the trigger point for growth—one can either stay still, hang onto the old feeling, or one can change."

At Long Last, Reality

At some point not long after the baby is born, just about every new father gets hit with a sharp jolt of reality: he's a father, with new responsibilities, new pressures, new expectations to live up to. For some new fathers, this seemingly basic epiphany comes early, before they leave the hospital. For others, reality may not hit for a few days. But whenever it happens, a new father's realization that his life has changed forever can have some interesting results.

Only a day after the birth of his daughter, Hannah, Ken Canfield pulled into his driveway. "I . . . stared out through the windshield at the wooden steps leading up into our house," he writes in *The Heart of a Father*. "The steps were rickety. One board was a little rotten on one end, and the rusty nails had gouged their way to the surface. Another board had warped up off the supports. I had never given any thought to those steps before . . . but the thought occurred to me that in less than 48 hours, a new mother carrying a new baby would be climbing those rickety stairs. So, exhausted as I was, with blood-shot eyes and the aroma of my sleepless hospital visit about me, I got out the power saw, some wood, a handful of nails, a square, and a hammer. For the next three hours I built steps."

You and Your Baby

Getting to Know Each Other

"Most people make babies out to be very complicated," says comedian Dave Barry, "but the truth is they have only three moods: Mood One: Just about to cry. Mood Two: Crying. Mood Three: Just finished crying. Your job, as a parent, is to keep the baby in Mood Three as much as possible." With just a few days of fatherhood under your belt you may be inclined to go along with Barry's summary. But the real truth is that babies' moods are a bit more subtle.

In the previous book in this series, *The Expectant Father: Facts, Tips, and Advice for Dads-to-Be*, I discussed the six clearly defined behavioral states that are evident within moments of every baby's birth. "By recognizing them and realizing when they occur and what the expected responses are in each," write Marshall and Phyllis Klaus, authors of *The Amazing Newborn*, "parents not only can get to know their infants but also can provide most sensitively for their needs."

In my first few weeks of fatherhood, I found that learning about these six states was absolutely critical to my getting to know my babies. So I thought it would be worthwhile to go over them again. Here, then, is a summary of the six states, based on the Klauses' wonderful book.

QUIET ALERT

Babies in the quiet alert state rarely move—all their energy is channeled into seeing and hearing. They can (and do) follow objects with their eyes and will even imitate your facial expressions.

Within the first hour of life, most infants have a period of quiet alertness that lasts an average of forty minutes. During his or her first week, the normal baby spends only about 10 percent of any twenty-four-hour period in this state. It is in this state, however, that your baby is most curious and is absorbing information about his or her new world. And while the baby is in this state, you will first become highly aware that there's a real person inside that tiny body.

ACTIVE ALERT

In the active alert state, the baby will make small sounds and move his or her arms, head, body, face, and eyes frequently and actively.

The baby's movements usually come in short bursts—a few seconds of activity every minute or two. Some researchers say these movements are designed to give parents subtle clues about what the baby wants and needs. Others say these movements are just interesting to watch, and therefore promote parent–infant interaction.

CRYING

Crying is a perfectly natural—and for some, frequent—state (for more on this, see pages 39, 42–45). The infant's eyes may be open or closed, the face red, and the arms and legs moving vigorously.

Often just picking up the baby and walking around with him or her will stop the crying. Interestingly, researchers used to think that babies were soothed by being held or rocked in the upright position. It turns out, though, that what makes them stop crying is not *being* upright, but the movement that gets them there.

Keep in mind, too, that crying is not a bad thing—it not only allows the baby to communicate but also provides valuable exercise. So if your efforts to calm aren't immediately successful (and the baby isn't hungry or stewing in a dirty diaper), don't worry; chances are the tears will stop by themselves in a few minutes.

DROWSINESS

Drowsiness is a transition state that occurs as the baby is waking up or falling asleep. There may still be some movement, and the eyes will often look dull or unfocused. Leave the baby alone to drift off to sleep or move into one of the alert stages.

QUIET SLEEP

During quiet sleep the baby's face is relaxed and the eyelids are closed and still. There are no body movements and only tiny, almost imperceptible mouth movements.

When your baby is in this state, you may be alarmed at the lack of movement and be afraid she has stopped breathing. If so, lean as close as you can and listen for the baby's breath. Otherwise, gently put a hand on the baby's stomach (if she's sleeping on her back) or back (if she's sleeping on her stomach) and feel it rise and fall. (For information on back versus stomach sleeping, see page 69.) Try to resist the urge to wake the baby up—most newborns spend up to 90 percent of their first few weeks sleeping.

ACTIVE SLEEP

Eyes are usually closed, but may occasionally flicker open. The baby may also smile or frown, make sucking or chewing movements, and even whimper or twitch—just as adults do in their active sleep state.

Half of a baby's sleep time is spent in quiet sleep, the other half in active sleep, with the two states alternating in thirty-minute shifts. So, if your sleeping baby starts to stir, whimper, or seems to be waking up unhappy, wait a few seconds before you pick him up to feed, change, or hold. Left alone, he may well slip back into the quiet sleep state.

Newborn babies are capable of a lot more than crying, sleeping, filling their diapers, and looking around. Just a few hours out of the womb, they are already trying to communicate with those around them. They can imitate facial expressions, have some control over their bodies, can express preferences (such as for simple patterns over more complex ones), and have remarkable memories.

Marshall Klaus describes playing a game with an eight-hour-old girl in which he asked one colleague (who was a stranger to the baby) to stick out her tongue slowly while holding the baby. After a few seconds, the baby imitated the woman. Then Dr. Klaus took the baby and passed her around to twelve other doctors and nurses who were participating in the game, all of whom were told not to stick their tongues out. When the baby finally came back to the first doctor, the baby—without any prompting—immediately stuck out her tongue again. Even at just a few hours old, she had apparently remembered her "friend."

Interacting with the Baby

Although it may be tempting just to sit and stare at your baby, marveling at every little thing she does, you'll need to do a lot more than that if you're really going to get to know her. Here are some of the best ways to get to know your child:

♦ **Hold her.** Newborns love to be carried around, whether held in your arms or in a pack.
♦ **Talk to her.** No, she can't understand a word you're saying. In fact, she barely even knows you exist. But talk to her anyway—explain everything

you're doing as you're doing it, tell her what's happening in the news, and so forth—it will help her get to know the rhythm of the language.

♦ **Change his diapers.** It doesn't sound like much fun, but it's a great time to interact with the baby one on one, to rub his soft belly, tickle his knees, kiss his tiny fingers. For at least the first month or so, he needs to be changed every two hours—a baby's super-sensitive skin shouldn't stew in human waste—so there are plenty of opportunities. And don't worry: changing diapers is an acquired skill; in just a few days you'll be able to do it with your eyes closed (although you probably shouldn't). In the mean-time, even if you don't do it right, baby stool washes right off your hands and won't stain your clothes. One hint, though: immediately after undoing the diaper, put something (such as a towel or cloth diaper) over baby for a few seconds. The sudden rush of fresh air on the baby's crotch can result in your getting sprayed.

A Note on Diapers and Wipers

It seems as though you can hardly do anything anymore without having to make choices—do you want the Tastes Great kind of beer or the Less Filling kind? do you want toothpaste with tartar control or with peroxide and baking soda? Fortunately, most of the choices we make are pretty easy. But some come with their very own built-in political controversy: Death penalty or life in prison? Smoking or non-smoking? Paper or plastic? Well, now that you're a parent, you can add "Disposable diapers or cloth?" to your list.

Americans throw away some eighteen billion disposable diapers a year, enough to constitute more than 1 percent of the nation's landfill. Disposables are made of plastic and will stay in their present form for about five hundred years. "Biodegradable" disposables are available in some places, but some environmentalists have complained that they use *more* plastic than the regular kind and take just as long to break down.

Cloth diapers, in contrast, are all natural. The problem is that they're made of cotton, which is taxing on farmland. And in order to sterilize cloth diapers properly, diaper services wash them seven times in near-boiling water, con-suming huge amounts of power, water, and chemical detergents. The diapers are then delivered all over town in trucks that fill the air with toxic pollutants. One study concluded that "use of a diaper service appears to consume three times as much fuel and cause nine times as much air pollution as use of disposable diapers."

Tough choice, and it's all yours.

And let's not forget the cost factor:

♦ **Disposable diapers:** $8 to $9 for a package of forty-four newborn size. As your baby and his diapers get bigger, the number of diapers per package goes down, but the cost per package stays about the same. Since you'll be using 5 to 8 diapers a day, this option can get pretty pricey. But if you keep your eyes out for coupons (most parenting magazines have a bunch of them in every issue), you can save a lot. In addition, places like Toys "Я" Us have generic or house brands that are a lot cheaper and usually just as good.

Some people say that kids who grow up with disposable diapers tend to become potty trained later than those who use cloth. Apparently, the disposable kind keep so much moisture away from the baby's bottom that the baby stays comfortable for a longer time.

♦ **Cloth diapers:** about $12 for a package of six. The availability and cost of diaper cleaning services vary greatly around the country. If you sign up with a diaper service, you'll probably start with about eighty diapers per week. If you're doing your own laundry, you should buy about forty.

Even if you decide against using cloth diapers for the baby, buy a dozen anyway—they're great for drying baby bottoms on changing tables and for draping over your shoulder to protect your clothes when your baby spits up.

Whichever you choose, make sure you stay away from commercial baby wipes for the first few weeks; they contain too many chemicals for brand-new skin. Use warm, wet washcloths instead. If you're taking the baby out during this period, bring along some moistened disposable washcloths in a resealable plastic bag. Finally, skip the lotions for a few weeks (again, too many chemicals and potential allergens) and never, never use powders (besides being a carcinogen, powder can cause pneumonia if inhaled).

If you happen to have been raised in a family that doesn't think a baby is properly changed unless her bottom is covered in white powder, try using cornstarch. Some people find that corn starch (which doesn't have the same health hazards as traditional baby powder) absorbs moisture and reduces diaper rash. But remember, you're not baking a cake here: a little goes a long way.

What about Play?

During the first few weeks, forget about football and chess. But try to spend at least twenty minutes a day (in five-minute installments) doing something with the baby one on one. Chatting, reading aloud, rocking, making faces,

> ## Different Isn't Bad, It's Just Different
>
> From the moment their children are born, men and women have very different ways of handling them. Men tend to stress the physical and high-energy more, women the social and emotional. Your baby will catch on to these differences within days, and she'll begin to react to you and your partner very differently. When she's hungry, she'll be more easily soothed by your partner (if she's breastfeeding), but she'll be happier to see you if she wants some physical stimulation. Don't let anyone tell you that the "guy things" you do are somehow not as important as the "girl things" your partner may do (or want *you* to do). Ultimately your baby needs both kinds of interactions, and it's a waste of time to try to compare or rate them. Just be gentle.

experimenting with the baby's reflexes (see pages 38–43) or even simply catching her gaze and looking into her eyes are great activities. Here are a couple of things to remember:

♦ **Take your cues from the baby.** If she cries or seems bored, stop what you're doing. Too much playing can make your child fussy or irritable, so limit play sessions to five minutes or so.

♦ **Schedule your fun.** The best time for physical play is when the baby is in the active alert state; playing with toys or books is fine during the quiet alert state (see page 17). Also, choose a time when your full attention can be devoted to the baby—no phone calls or other distractions.

♦ **Be encouraging.** Use lots of smiles and laughter as well as verbal encouragement. Although the baby can't understand the words, she definitely understands the feelings. Even at only a few days old, she'll want to please you, and lots of reinforcement will help build her self-confidence.

♦ **Be gentle.** Because babies' heads are relatively large (one-quarter of their body size at birth versus one-seventh by the time they're adults) and their neck muscles are not yet well developed, their heads tend to be pretty floppy for the first few months. Be sure to support the head from behind at all times, and avoid sudden or jerky motions. *Never* shake your child. This can make their little brains rattle around inside their skulls, causing bruises or permanent injuries. Never throw the baby up in the air. Yes, your father may have done it to you, but he shouldn't have. It looks like fun but can be extremely dangerous.

Family Matters

Coming Home

Boy, has your life changed. You're still your partner's lover and friend, just as you were a few weeks ago, but now, of course, you're also a father. You may be worried about how you're going to juggle all your various roles, but for a few days the most important thing you can do is to be a solid support person to your partner. Besides her physical recovery (which we'll talk more about below), she's going to need time to get to know the baby and to learn (if she chooses to) how to breastfeed.

Your first days as a father will be awfully busy—mine sure were: cooking, shopping, doing laundry, fixing up the baby's room, getting the word out, screening phone calls and visitors, and making sure my partner got plenty of rest.

Recovery

As far as the baby is concerned, there's not much to do in the beginning besides feeding, changing, and admiring. But your partner is a different story. Despite whatever you've heard about women giving birth in the fields and returning to work a few minutes later, that's not the way things usually happen. Having a baby is a major shock—physically and emotionally—to a woman's system. And, contrary to popular belief, the recovery period after a vaginal birth is not necessarily any shorter or easier than the recovery period after a C-section. In fact, my wife—who has delivered both ways—says recovering from the C-section was a lot easier.

Physically, whatever kind of delivery your partner has, she'll need some time—probably more than either of you think—to recover fully. Fatigue, breast soreness, and lingering uterine contractions may not disappear for months, and vaginal discomfort, hemorrhoids, poor appetite, constipation, increased perspiration, acne, hand numbness or tingling, dizziness, and hot flashes may continue for weeks after delivery. In addition, between 10 and 40 percent of women feel pain during sexual intercourse (which they won't get around to for a few months anyway, so don't bother thinking about it), have respiratory infections, and lose hair for three to six months.

Emotionally, your partner isn't much better off. She's likely to be a little impatient at her lack of mobility, and while she's undoubtedly excited to be a mother and relieved that the pregnancy is finally over, she may well experience at least some postpartum depression (see pages 45–47). Now that the baby

Pets

Don't expect your pet to be as excited as you are about the birth of your baby; many dogs and cats do not appreciate their new (lower) status in your house. To minimize the trauma for your pet (and to minimize the chance your pet will do something to harm the baby), try to get your pet used to the baby as early as possible.

You can do this even before the baby comes home by putting a blanket in the baby's bassinet in the hospital, then rushing the blanket home to your pet. It'll give Rover or Fluffy a few days (or hours, at least) to get used to the interloper's smell.

"Homewrecker!"

is really here, she may feel a lot of pressure to assume her new role as mother and to breastfeed properly. Fortunately, as she and the baby get to know each other, her confidence will grow and a lot of her anxieties should disappear.

Here are some things you can do to make the recovery process as easy as possible and to start parenting off on the right foot:

♦ Help your partner resist the urge to do too much too soon.

♦ Take over the household chores or ask someone else to help. And if the house is a mess, don't blame each other.

Parents, In-Laws, Siblings, and Other "Helpers"

One of the most common questions you'll hear from people is whether they can help out in any way. Some people are serious; others are just being polite. You can tell one group from the other by keeping a list of chores that need to be done and asking them to take their pick.

Be particularly careful about accepting offers of help from people—especially parents (yours or hers)—who arrive on your doorstep with suitcases and open-ended travel arrangements. New grandparents may have more traditional attitudes toward parenting and may not be supportive of your involvement with your child. They may also have very different ideas about how babies should be fed, dressed, carried, played with, and so on.

The same can be said for just about anyone else who offers to move in with you for a few days, weeks, or months to "help out," especially people who have their own kids. With all your other responsibilities, the last thing you want to do is play host to a bunch of relatives. If someone does stay with you to help out after the birth, make sure he or she understands that although you appreciate their help and their suggestions, you and your partner are the baby's parents and what the two of you say ultimately goes.

♦ Be flexible. Expecting to maintain your normal, prefatherhood schedule is unrealistic, especially for the first six weeks after the birth.
♦ Be patient with yourself, your partner, and the baby. You're all new at this.
♦ Be sensitive to your partner's emotions. Her emotional recovery can take just as long as her physical one.
♦ Make sure to get some time alone with the baby. You can do this while your partner is sleeping or, if you have to, while you send her out for a walk.
♦ Control the visiting hours and the number of people who can come at any given time. Dealing with visitors takes a lot more energy than you might think. And being poked, prodded, and passed around won't make the baby very happy. Also, for the first month or so, ask anyone who wants to touch the baby to wash his or her hands first.
♦ Keep your sense of humor.

Feeding the Baby: Breast versus Bottle

At the time most of the people reading this book were born, breastfeeding was out of style and most women our mothers' age were given a wide variety of reasons (by their doctors, of course) not to breastfeed. But in the nineties you'd be hard-pressed to find anyone in the medical community who doesn't agree that breast-feeding is just about the best thing you can do for your child. Here's why:

FOR THE BABY

♦ Breast milk provides exactly the right balance of nutrients needed by your newborn. In addition, breast milk contains several essential fatty acids that are not found in baby formula.

♦ Breast milk adapts, as if by magic, to your baby's changing nutritional needs. Neither of our children had a single sip of anything but breast milk for the first seven or eight months of life, and they're both wonderfully healthy kids.

Just Because You Don't Have Breasts Doesn't Mean You Can't Help Breastfeed

Sounds strange, but *you* play a major role in determining how long—and how well—your partner will breastfeed. Several studies have shown that women breastfeed longer when their partners learn about breastfeeding (which you'll do as you read these pages). And English breastfeeding expert Sheila Kitzinger has found that besides learning, the father's support and confidence in his partner are decisive factors in the mother's desire and ability to breastfeed.

+ Breastfeeding greatly reduces the chance that your baby will develop food allergies. If either of your families has a history of food allergies, you should withhold solid foods for at least six months.
+ Breastfed babies are less prone to obesity in adulthood than formula-fed babies. This may be because with the breast it's the baby—not the parent—who decides when to quit eating.
+ Breastfed babies have a greatly reduced risk of developing respiratory and gastrointestinal illness.
+ Breastfeeding is thought to transmit to the infant the mother's immunity to certain diseases.

Just Because Your Partner Has Breasts Doesn't Mean She Knows How to Use Them

As natural as breastfeeding appears to be, your partner and the baby may need anywhere from a few days to a few weeks to get the hang of it. The baby won't immediately know how to latch on to the breast properly, and your partner—never having done this before—won't know exactly what to do either. This initial period, in which cracked and even bloody nipples are not uncommon, may be quite painful for your partner. And with the baby feeding six or seven times a day, it may take as long as two weeks for your partner's nipples to get sufficiently toughened up.

Surprisingly, your partner won't begin producing any real milk until two to five days after the baby is born. But there's no need to worry that the baby isn't getting enough food. Babies don't eat much the first 24–48 hours, and any sucking they do is almost purely for practice. Whatever nutritional needs your baby has will be fully satisfied by the tiny amounts of colostrum your partner produces. (Colostrum is a kind of premilk that helps the baby's immature digestive system get warmed up for the task of digesting real milk later.)

Overall, the first few weeks of breastfeeding can be very stressful for your partner. If this is the case, do not be tempted to suggest switching to bottles. Instead, be supportive, praise her for the great job she's doing, bring her something to eat or drink while she's feeding, and encourage her to keep trying. You also might ask your pediatrician for the name of a local lactation consultant (what a job!).

FOR YOU AND YOUR PARTNER

♦ It's convenient—no preparation, no heating, no bottles or dishes to wash . . .

♦ It's free. Formula can cost a lot of money.

♦ It gives your partner a wonderful opportunity to bond with the baby. In addition, breastfeeding will help get your partner's uterus back into shape and may reduce her risk of both ovarian and breast cancer.

♦ In most cases, there's always as much as you need, and never any waste.

♦ Your baby's diapers won't stink. It's true. Breastfed babies produce stool that—especially when compared to formula stools—doesn't smell half bad.

What If Your Partner Doesn't Breastfeed

JUICE

If you and your partner decide not to breastfeed or decide to supplement breastfeeding with a bottle, don't fill it with juice. A recent study found that children who drink large quantities of fruit juice—especially apple juice— suffer from frequent diarrhea and, in the worst cases, may fail to grow and develop normally. The problem is that babies love juice so much that, if you give them all they want, they'll fill up their tiny stomachs with it, leaving no room for the more nutritious foods they need. The American Dietetic Association recommends that parents refrain from giving their babies juice until they're at least six months old, and then restrict juice intake until age two.

FORMULA

Prices vary. You can use powdered, full-strength liquid, or liquid concentrate. But when you start checking formula prices, your partner may decide to keep breastfeeding a while longer. When we weaned our older daughter, we put her on the powdered formula; I made a pitcher of it every morning and kept it in the refrigerator.

A Few Cosmetic Details

SKIN

Before my first daughter was born, I'm pretty sure that I believed that she— even right after her birth—would look radiant and have clear, glowing skin. Well, chalk up another victory for the ad execs. The fact is that in most cases, babies' skin isn't radiant or clear. But before you panic and call a dermatologist, here are some of the more common, and perfectly normal, newborn skin conditions you should know about:

♦ **Acne.** These cute little pimples are usually confined to the baby's face and are either the result of your partner's hormones continuing to swim through the baby's system or of his underdeveloped pores. Either way, don't squeeze, poke, pick at, or scrub these pimples. Just wash them with water a few times a day, pat them dry, and they'll go away in a few months.

♦ **Blisters.** Pictures taken of babies in utero have shown that long before birth, they frequently suck their thumbs—or any other part of their body they can reach. Sometimes they suck so hard they raise blisters.

♦ **Jaundice.** If your baby's skin and/or the whites of his eyes seem a little yellow, he may have jaundice. This condition is the result of the baby's liver being unable adequately to process bilirubin, a yellowish by-product of red blood cells. It affects about 25 percent of newborns (and a higher percentage of preemies), appears within the first five days of life, and is usually gone a few days later.

♦ **Splotches, blotches, birthmarks.** They can be white, purple, brown, or even yellow with white bumps in the center, and they can appear on the face, legs, arms, back. In most cases, they'll go away on their own if you just leave them alone. But if you're really worried, check with your pediatrician.

♦ **Cradle cap.** Also called seborrheic dermatitis, cradle cap looks like flaky, yellowish, sometimes greasy dandruff. It usually shows up on the head, but can also work its way into baby's eyebrows. It isn't a serious condition and will bother you much more than it does the baby. Frequent shampooing with a baby shampoo will help it go away.

CLEANING

Your baby's umbilical cord stump will drop off anywhere from one to three weeks after she's born. Until then, limit your baby-washing efforts to sponge baths. Keep the stump as dry as possible and clean it with rubbing alcohol on a cotton swab every time you change her diaper. Folding down the front of the diaper exposes the stump to more air and speeds up the falling-off process.

Until your baby starts moving around by herself, don't bathe her any more often than three times a week. (You may take a shower every day, but until she starts crawling, she's unlikely to do anything that would get her terribly dirty.) Any more than that could unnecessarily dry her skin. A few exceptions: it's okay to clean the baby's face every day, and be sure to carefully clean everything covered up by her diapers every time you change one.

For Boys Only

I'm assuming that by now, you and your partner have already made your decision about whether or not to circumcise your son. Whatever your choice, your son's penis requires some special care.

THE CIRCUMCISED PENIS

The penis will be red and sore for a few days after the circumcision. Until it's fully healed, you'll need to protect the newly exposed tip and keep it from sticking to the inside of his diaper (a few tiny spots of blood on his diapers for a few days, however, is perfectly normal). Ordinarily, you'll need to keep the penis dry, and the tip lubricated with petroleum jelly or antibiotic ointment and wrapped in gauze to protect it from urine, which is very irritating. The person who performed the circumcision or the hospital nursing staff will be able to tell you how long to keep the penis covered and how often to change the bandages.

THE UNCIRCUMCISED PENIS

Even if you elect not to circumcise your son, you'll still have to spend some time taking care of his penis. The standard way to clean an uncircumcised penis is to retract the foreskin and gently wash the head of the penis with mild soap and water. However, 85 percent of boys under six months have foreskins that don't retract, according to the American Academy of Pediatrics. If this is the case with your son, do not force it. Check with your pediatrician immediately and follow his or her hygiene instructions carefully. Fortunately, as boys get older, their foreskins retract on their own; by age one, 50 percent retract, and by age three, 80 to 90 percent.

Notes:

Getting to Know You

What's Going On with the Baby

Physically

♦ Most of your baby's physical movements are still reflexive. But sometime this month, while flailing his arms around he'll accidentally stick his hand into his mouth. After getting over the initial shock, your baby will realize that sucking—even when there's no milk involved—is downright fun. By the end of the month, he'll probably be able to get his hand in his mouth—on purpose—fairly regularly.

♦ Lying on his tummy, he's now able to lift his head just enough to turn it so his nose won't be smashed into the mattress.

♦ If you put him in a sitting position, he'll try to keep his head in line with his back, but he won't be able to hold it steady for more than a second or two without support.

♦ Waste production is way down: 2 to 3 bowel movements and 5 to 6 wet diapers per day.

Intellectually

♦ Your baby is already beginning to express an interest in finding out what's new in the world—he'll stare at a new object for much longer than a familiar one.

♦ According to psychiatrist Peter Wolff, an object exists for a baby only as "something to suck, or something to see, or something to grasp, but not as something to grasp *and* to see at the same time."

Verbally

- As his vocal chords mature, your baby will be able to expand his collection of animal sounds to include some small, throaty, and incredibly cute noises.
- He is already beginning to differentiate between language and the other kinds of noise he hears all day.
- Still, his main form of using his vocal chords will be to cry—something he'll do for a total of about three hours a day.

Emotionally/Socially

- Don't expect many hints from your baby about what he's thinking—most of the time his expression is pretty blank.
- Not quite ready for the cocktail circuit, your baby is probably sleeping 16 to 20 hours a day. In fact, he may use sleep as a kind of self-defense mechanism, shutting down his systems when he gets overstimulated.

What You're Going Through

Bonding with the Baby

In one of the earliest studies of father-infant interaction, researcher Ross Parke made a discovery that shocked a lot of traditionalists: fathers were just as caring, interested, and involved with their infants as mothers were, and they held, touched, kissed, rocked, and cooed at their new babies with at least the same frequency as mothers did. Several years later, Dr. Martin Greenberg coined a term, *engrossment,* to describe "a father's sense of absorption, pre-occupation, and interest in his baby."

Over the years a number of other researchers have confirmed these findings about father-infant interaction and have concluded that what triggers engrossment in men is the same thing that prompts similar nurturing feelings in women: early infant contact. "In sum," writes Dr. Parke, "the amount of stimulatory and affectional behavior depends on the opportunity to hold the infant."

Not surprisingly, Parke and others have found that men who attended their babies' birth bonded slightly faster than those who didn't. But if you weren't able to be there for the birth, don't worry. "Early contact at birth is not a magic pill," writes Ellen Galinsky. "It does not guarantee attachment. Neither does lack of contact prevent bonding."

But What If I Don't Bond Right Away?

If you haven't established an instant bond with your baby, there's absolutely nothing wrong with you. In fact, in a study by psychiatrists Kay Robson and

Remesh Kumar, 25 to 40 percent of new parents—mothers *and* fathers—admitted that their first response to the baby was "indifference." Putting it in slightly stronger terms, researcher Katherine May says, "This bonding business is nonsense. We've sold parents a bill of goods. They believe that if they don't have skin-to-skin contact within the first fifteen minutes, they won't bond. Science just doesn't show that."

This really makes more sense than the love-at-first-sight kind of bonding you hear so much about. And anyway, there's no evidence whatsoever that your relationship with or feelings for your child will be any less loving than if you'd fallen head over heels in love in the first second. So, just take your time. Don't pressure yourself, and don't think for a second that you've failed as a father.

In addition, there's a lot of evidence that parent-child bonding comes as a result of physical closeness. So if you'd like to speed up the process, try carrying the baby every chance you get, taking him with you whenever you can, and taking care of as many of his basic needs as possible.

My Baby Doesn't Love Me

For about the first six to eight weeks of life, your baby probably won't give you much feedback about how you're doing as a father: he won't smile, laugh, or react to you in any noticeable way. In fact, just about all he will do is cry. This can result in your feeling unloved and, surprisingly often, feeling a need to "get even" with the baby by deliberately withholding your own love.

As the grown-up, it's your job to nip this destructive cycle in the bud. "The relationship between parent and child is interactive," writes Ellen Galinsky. "What the child does affects what the parent does, which in turn affects what the child does." So if you find yourself feeling unloved or unappreciated by your newborn, here are a few things to keep in mind:

♦ Although your baby can express preferences for sounds, tastes, or patterns (see pages 13–14, 19), he is not yet capable of expressing love.
♦ Your baby's needs and wants are fairly limited at this stage—feed me, change me, hold me, put me in bed—and he has a different way of letting you know which one he wants. If you pay close attention, you'll soon be able to figure out what he's "telling" you. Getting to know your baby in this way will make you feel less anxious and more confident as a parent, which will make the baby more comfortable with you, which in turn will make your mutual attachment more secure.
♦ Another important way to get to know your baby is by carefully reading the "What's Going On with the Baby" sections of this book. Knowing what your baby is capable of—and what he isn't—at various stages can go a long way

Attachment and Bonding Are *Not* the Same Thing

While there's no question that bonding with your baby is an important goal, it is essentially a one-way street: you establish a relationship with the infant and don't get much back. But attachment is more of a two-way street: you and the baby establish relationships with each other.

In our attachment relationships with adults (including our partners), both players have "relatively equal positions in providing an emotionally satisfying relationship with each other," write Barbara and Philip Newman of Ohio State University. But the attachment you have with your baby is not—by any stretch of the imagination—equal. It is, however, balanced in very interesting and delicate ways.

Basically, it works like this: as you learn to read your baby's signals and satisfy his needs in an appropriate way, he learns to view you as a reliable and responsive person—someone he can count on in times of trouble. And he'll find some way (babies always do) to get you the message that you're needed and wanted.

This exchange of information is what psychologist Bertrand Cramer and pediatrician T. Berry Brazelton call "synchronous communication." And according to them, parents who have synchronous communication with their babies "experience their own competence. . . . When they achieve it for themselves, the most insecure parents can feel a sense of control, over their baby's vulnerabilities and over their own."

Meanwhile, babies who have synchronous "chats" with their parents come to prefer them over any of the other adults around who might be able to satisfy a need or two. Over time, this kind of preference (based on feelings of security and the parents' reliability) develops into self-confidence and becomes the foundation for all of the growing baby's future relationships.

toward helping you understand your baby's behavior and establish reasonable expectations.

♦ Change your perspective a little. The fact that your baby often stops crying when you pick him up and that he loves to fall asleep on your chest are signs that he feels close to you and trusts you—critical steps on the way to the love you want him to feel. Allow yourself the pleasure of stroking his incredibly soft skin, of admiring his tiny fingers, and of filling your lungs with his clean, new baby smell. If that doesn't hook you, nothing will.

Bonding, Attachment, and Adoptive Parents

It's extremely common for adoptive couples—particularly those who adopted because of infertility—to feel insecure or inadequate as parents. They often believe that the process of bonding and forming an attachment with a baby comes "naturally" to birth parents, and that since they weren't with the baby from the beginning, they'll never be as close to their child as a biological parent would.

The good news is that this isn't true. "Most infants, if adopted before the age of nine months," write adoption psychotherapists Judith Schaffer and Christina Lindstrom, "will take to their new parents as if they were born to them, developing an attachment to them as they would have done to their birth parents."

There are things, of course, that can interfere with adoptive parent-child attachment. Among the most common are the feelings of inadequacy discussed above, and the age and physical health of the child at adoption. But remember: as we've discussed earlier in this chapter, the processes of bonding and attachment don't happen automatically. They take time—and often a lot of work—to develop. In all but the rarest cases, the desire for attachment to a child can overcome even the most formidable obstacles.

So if you're worried for any reason about your abilities as a parent or about anything else that might get in the way of your relationship with your adopted child, call the National Adoption Information Clearinghouse, at (301) 231-6512, or The National Adoption Center, at (800) TO-ADOPT. Either of these organizations can refer you to resources—including support groups and counseling services—in your area. A few other adoption-related resources are listed in the Resources appendix of this book.

The Incredible Shrinking Baby

In their first week or so of life, most babies lose some weight—often as much as 25 percent of their birth weight. This can be pretty scary, especially since babies are generally supposed to get bigger over time, not smaller. This shrinking baby thing is perfectly normal (in the first few days the baby isn't eating much), and your baby will probably regain his birth weight by the time he's two weeks old. After that, the rate of growth—for the next few months, at least—is phenomenal: about an ounce a day and an inch per month. Doesn't sound like much, but if he continued growing at this rate, by his eighteenth birthday your baby would be nearly twenty feet tall and weigh in at about 420 pounds.

During every visit to the pediatrician your baby will be weighed, his overall length and head circumference will be measured, and the results will be given not only in inches (or centimeters) but in *percentile.* (If your baby is in the 75th percentile for weight, that means that he's heavier than 75 percent of babies the same age.) Try not to get too caught up with these numbers. As with most things, bigger isn't necessarily better; more important, it's normal for different parts of a baby's body to grow at different rates. Both my daughters, for example, were built like nails—90th percentile for both height and head size, but 40th percentile for weight.

Keep in mind also that the numbers on these charts generally apply to formula-fed babies, who tend to bulk up a little more quickly than their breastfed agemates.

You and Your Baby

The most important thing you can do for your baby is to make him feel loved and cared for. And the best way to do this is to continue to do the activities listed on pages 19–20, only more so.

Reading
At this age, you can read just about anything to your baby—even *War and Peace* or those *New Yorker* profiles you're so behind on. "What is important . . . is that the child becomes accustomed to the rhythmic sounds of your reading voice and associates it with a peaceful, secure time of day," writes Jim Trelease, author of *The New Read Aloud Handbook.* So set up a regular reading time and place. And as with most baby-related things, your baby will let you know whether she's interested or not, so don't force her to sit through the end of a chapter.

Toys and Games
Giving your baby a rattle, stuffed animal, or anything else that needs to be grasped is a total waste of time. She simply isn't interested in toys right now. That doesn't mean, however, that she doesn't want to play. If you pay close attention, you'll soon figure out when she's telling you she wants to play. "She'll look you straight in the eye and 'talk' to you," write Drs. Art Ulene and Steven Shelov. "The talk may be only a syllable or two, or it may be a

"You have the right to remain silent . . ."

prolonged cooing, but you'll know from the tone and intensity whether she's in a good mood or a bad."

It's even more important that you learn to recognize the clues your baby gives you when she wants to quit. "At first she'll look away," say Ulene and Shelov. "Then she may become glassy-eyed or look right through you. She may move her body to physically turn away or simply go limp. Finally, if all else fails, she may wail for escape. By getting to know and respect your baby's early warning signals, you can spare both of you a lot of needless discomfort."

Visual Stimulation

Since your baby still isn't capable of grabbing hold of much of anything, she's doing most of her learning with her eyes. Here are a few ways to stimulate your baby visually:

- ♦ Fasten an unbreakable mirror securely to the inside of the baby's crib.
- ♦ Make sure the baby has a lot of different things to look at. For the first few months, infants are particularly responsive to high contrast, so black-and-white toys and patterns are often a big hit.
- ♦ Have your baby show you what she prefers. Hold up different patterns

12 to 18 inches from the baby's face for a few seconds. Which ones does she stare at intently? Which ones does she turn away from?

♦ Play some visual tracking games. With the baby on his back, hold a small object 12 to 18 inches from his nose. Move the object slowly to one side. Does the baby follow the object with his eyes? Does he move his head? Do the same thing for the other side.

Whatever games you're playing with the baby, keep in mind that your baby is not a trained seal and that these activities are games, not college entrance exams.

Mobiles

Mobiles are among the most popular furnishings in almost any baby's room. And this is the perfect time to put some up: one over the bed and perhaps another, smaller one over the changing table. When considering mobiles, keep these ideas in mind:

♦ Get mobiles that allow you to change the figures. As your baby gets older his taste will become more sophisticated and you'll need to keep up. My wife and I found that mobile characters were quite expensive; we could have bought a year's worth of clothes for the baby with what it would have cost us to buy five or six sets of mobile characters. The solution? Make your own.

♦ When buying or making mobile characters, keep in mind that the baby will be looking at them from underneath. Quite a number of manufacturers produce mobiles that are gorgeous when viewed from the parents' perspective, but from the baby's perspective they're essentially blank.

♦ At this point, your baby is still interested in simple lines: stripes, large squares, and the outlines of things. Intricate patterns or complicated designs are not appropriate now.

♦ Keep the mobile 6 to 18 inches above the baby's face and put it slightly to the side; babies don't like to look straight up for long.

Fun with Reflexes

"The newborn is faced with two fundamental and simultaneous challenges during the first weeks of life," writes child psychiatrist Stanley I. Greenspan. "The first is self-regulation—the ability to feel calm and relaxed, not overwhelmed by his new environment. The second is to become interested in the world about him."

Unfortunately, babies can't do much to accomplish either of these goals on their own. That's your job. And you'll do it by caring for and responding to your baby, and by providing him with a stimulating environment. But because your baby can't be expected to sit around waiting for you, he came fully equipped with a wide range of reflexes to get him started.

Yes, all that wild, seemingly random arm and leg flailing really has a purpose: "Many reflexes are designed to help infants to survive and lead them on to more complicated sequences of voluntary behavior," write the Newmans. "The sucking reflex is a good example. At birth, inserting something in an infant's mouth produces the sucking reflex. This reflex helps infants gain nourishment relatively easily before sucking behavior is under voluntary control."

Understanding these reflexes can give you greater insight into your baby's behavior. And by keeping track of when they disappear, you'll be able to monitor his development. Best of all, they're a lot of fun—for you as well as the baby.

In addition to these reflexes, there are a few more that the experts haven't yet figured out what to do with. For example, babies seem able to determine the path of an oncoming object; they will take defensive action (leaning back hard, turning away, closing eyes, bringing arms up in front of the face) if the object is going to hit them. But if the object isn't on a path that will hit the baby, he'll ignore it. If you want to try this, strap your baby into his car seat and, from a few feet away, move a ball or other fairly large object straight at his head and again past him.

If you want to experiment with any of these reflexes, the best time is during your baby's active alert stage (see page 18). Remember to be extra careful of the baby's head and to respect his desire to quit.

Family Matters

Crying

Since the moment your baby was born she's been trying to communicate with you. That's the good news. The bad news is that she settled on crying as the way to do it. It will take you a while to teach her that there are more effective, and less annoying, ways of getting your attention. In the meantime, though, if she's like most babies, she's a real chatterbox: 80 to 90 percent of all babies have crying spells that last from twenty minutes to an hour every day.

Of course, not all of your baby's tears mean that she is sad, uncomfortable, or dissatisfied with something you've done. Nevertheless, holding an inconsolably crying baby can bring out a range of emotions, even in the most seasoned parent, running from pity and frustration to fury and inadequacy.

Exploring Your Baby's Reflexes

IF YOU	THE BABY WILL
◆ Tap the bridge of your baby's nose (gently, please), turn on a bright light, or clap your hands close to his head	◆ Close his eyes tightly
◆ Make a sudden, loud noise or give the baby the sensation of falling	◆ Fling legs and arms out and back, throw head back, open eyes wide, and cry
◆ Straighten the baby's arms and legs	◆ Flex arms and legs
◆ Pull baby up to a sitting position (be sure to support baby's head while doing this)	◆ Snap eyes open, tense shoulders, try (usually unsuccessfully) to right head
◆ Stand baby up (while holding under the arms) on a solid surface; works just as well holding baby against a wall (but be sure to support her head)	◆ Lift one leg, then the other, as if marching
◆ Put baby on tummy on flat surface or support baby's chest on a water surface (if trying in water, *do not let go*—baby can't really swim); *never do this on a beanbag or other soft surface—baby can suffocate*	◆ Turn head to side and lift it slightly; wiggle arms around as if swimming
◆ Stroke back of hand or top of foot; gently poke sole	◆ Withdraw hand or foot and arch it
◆ Stroke leg or upper body	◆ Cross opposite leg or hand to push hand away
◆ Stroke palm or sole of foot	◆ Grasp with hand or foot; hand grasp may be strong enough to allow you to pull baby to sitting position (be sure to support head)

WHAT IT MEANS	HOW LONG UNTIL IT'S GONE
◆ Protects baby's eyes from being injured by an object or a harsh light	◆ 1–2 months
◆ A fairly primitive way for the newborn to call for help	◆ Called the Moro or startle reflex, disappears within 3 or 4 months
◆ Probably the body's attempt to resist being held down	◆ 3 months
◆ Attempts to get self upright	◆ Called the China Doll reflex, disappears within 1–2 months
◆ Baby can protect herself by kicking away potentially dangerous things; has absolutely nothing to do with real walking	◆ About 2 months
◆ A way for the baby to protect self against smothering	◆ 2–4 months
◆ Protection against pain	◆ 2–4 months
◆ Protection against pain	◆ 3–4 months
◆ Encourages baby to start understanding the shape, texture, and weight of whatever she's grasping	◆ 2–4 months

(continued on next page)

Exploring Your Baby's Reflexes *(continued from pages 40–41)*

IF YOU	THE BABY WILL
♦ Stroke cheek or mouth	♦ Turn head toward side being stroked, open mouth and start sucking
♦ Place an object over baby's face (be *very careful* while doing this)	♦ Open and close mouth vigorously, twist head, flail arms
♦ Place baby on his back and turn his head to one side (don't force anything)	♦ Straighten arm on the side he is looking, bend arm and leg on other side

Fathers are likely to experience these feelings—especially inadequacy—more acutely than mothers. As with so many mother/father differences, the culprit is socialization: most men come into fatherhood feeling less than completely confident in their own parenting abilities, and a baby's cries are too easily seen as confirmation that daddy is doing a less-than-adequate job.

As difficult as crying can be to deal with, you obviously don't want your baby to be completely silent (in fact, if your baby doesn't cry at least several times a day, have a talk with your pediatrician). Fortunately, there are a few things you can do to make your baby's crying a less unpleasant experience for both of you:

♦ **When (not if) your child starts to cry, resist the urge to hand him or her to your partner.** She knows nothing more about crying babies than you do (or will soon enough). Since each of you instinctively has a different way of interacting with the baby, your hanging in there through a crying spell will double the chances you'll find new ways to soothe the baby.

♦ **Learn to speak your baby's language.** By now, you can almost always tell your baby's cry from any other baby's, and you can probably recognize her "I'm tired," "Feed me now," and "Change my diaper" cries. And while the language she speaks isn't as sexy or as vocabulary-rich as French, your baby has added a few more "phrases" to her vocabulary, including "I'm as uncomfortable as hell," "I'm bored out of my mind," and "I'm crying because I'm mad and I'm not going to stop no matter what you do." Responding promptly when your baby cries will help you learn to recognize which cry is which. You'll then be able to tailor your response and keep your baby happy.

♦ **Carry your baby more.** The more you hold them (even when they're not

WHAT IT MEANS	HOW LONG UNTIL IT'S GONE
◆ Called rooting reflex, helps baby get ready to eat	◆ 3–4 months
◆ Attempt to keep from suffocating	◆ 5–7 months
◆ Called the tonic neck reflex or fencer's pose, encourages baby to use each side of body and to notice own hands	◆ 1–3 months

crying), the less likely they are to cry. In one study, researchers found that a two-hour increase in carrying time per day resulted in a 42 percent decrease in crying time.

◆ **Get to know your baby's routine.** Keeping a diary of when your baby cries, how long the crying spells last, and what (if anything) works to slow them down can really help. Some babies like to thrash around and cry a little (or a lot) before going to sleep; others don't.

◆ **If your partner is breastfeeding, watch what she eats.** This is especially important if the baby suddenly and inexplicably deviates from her normal crying routine. Broccoli, cauliflower, brussels sprouts, and milk, when consumed by nursing mothers, often result in gastrically distressed (and weepy) babies.

After you've tried soothing, feeding, changing the diaper, checking for uncomfortable clothing, and rocking, the baby may still continue to howl. Sometimes there's really nothing you can do about it (see the section "Coping with Crying," pages 44–45), but sometimes all it takes is a new approach. Here are a few alternatives you might want to try:

◆ **Hold the baby differently.** Not all babies like to be held facing you; some want to face out so they can see the world. One of the most successful ways I've learned to soothe a crying baby—and I've tried this on many kids besides my own—is to use Dave's Magic Baby Hold. (Dave, the father of a close friend, supposedly used the Hold to calm his own three children.) Quite simply, have the baby "sit" in the palm of your hand—thumb in front, the other fingers on the baby's bottom. Then have the baby lie face down on the inside of your forearm, with his or her head resting on the inside of your elbow. Use your other hand to stroke or pat the baby's back.

- **Distraction.** Offer a toy, a story, a song. If the baby is diverted by a story or song, you'd better be prepared to repeat it over and over and over. . . .
- **Give the baby something to suck on.** Just take a guess why they call them "pacifiers." If you don't approve of pacifiers, you can either help the baby suck on his or her own fingers, or loan out one of yours (for more on pacifiers, see page 137).
- **Give the baby a bath.** Some babies find warm water soothing. Others freak out when they get wet. If you do decide to try bathing a crying infant, don't do it alone. Holding onto a calm soapy baby is no easy chore. Keeping a grip on a squirming, screaming, soapy baby takes a team of highly trained specialists.
- **Invest in a frontpack.** No matter how strong you think you are, carrying a baby around—even a newborn—is rough on the arms and back.
- **Take the baby for a walk or a drive.** A word of caution: this doesn't work for all babies. When she was an infant, my elder daughter would fall asleep in the stroller or the car in a heartbeat. But my younger daughter hates riding in the car, especially when she's tired, and cries even more when she's put in her car seat. If you don't feel like going out, try putting the baby on top of a running washing machine or dryer. There's also a special device called SleepTight that, when attached to the baby's crib, simulates the feel (and sounds) of a car going fifty-five miles an hour. Call 1-800-NO-COLIC for more information.

Coping with Crying

If you've tried everything you can think of to stop the baby from crying but to no avail, here are some things that may help you cope:

- **Tag-team crying duty.** There's no reason why both you and your partner have to suffer together through what Martin Greenberg calls "the tyranny of crying." Spelling each other in twenty-minute or half-hour shifts will do you both a world of good. Getting a little exercise during your "time off" will also calm your nerves before your next shift starts.
- **Let the baby "cry it out."** If the crying has gone on for more than twenty minutes, you might put the baby in his crib and give yourself a break. If the baby doesn't stop screaming in ten minutes, pick him up and try to soothe him some other way for fifteen more minutes. Repeat as necessary. Note: The "crying it out" approach should be used only after you've tried everything else. Generally speaking, you should respond promptly and

"See what Daddy has for you, if you stop crying?"

lovingly to your baby's cries. Several studies show that babies who are responded to in this way develop into more confident youngsters.

♦ **Get some help.** Dealing with a crying child for even a few minutes can provoke incredible rage and frustration. And if the screams go on for hours, it can become truly difficult to maintain your sanity, let alone control your temper. If you find yourself concerned that you might lash out (other than verbally) at your child, call someone: your partner, pediatrician, parents, baby-sitter, friends, neighbors, clergy person, or even a parental-stress hotline. If your baby is a real crier, keep these numbers handy.

♦ **Don't take it personally.** Your baby isn't deliberately trying to antagonize you. It's all too easy to let your frustration at this temporary situation permanently interfere with the way you treat your child. "Even if your powerful feelings don't lead to child abuse," write the authors of *What to Expect the First Year*, "they can start eroding your relationship with your baby and your confidence in yourself as a parent unless you get counseling quickly."

Dealing with Postpartum Blues and Depression

About 70 percent of new mothers experience periods of mild sadness, weepiness, moodiness, sleep deprivation, loss of appetite, inability to make decisions, anger, or anxiety after the baby is born. These postpartum blues, which many

Colic

Starting at about two weeks of age, some 10–20 percent of babies develop colic—crying spells that, unlike "ordinary" crying, can last for hours at a time. Although many colicky babies limit their crying to certain times of the day, many others cry all day or all night. The duration and intensity of crying spells peaks at about six weeks, and usually disappears entirely within three months.

Since there's no real agreement on what causes colic or on what to do about it, your pediatrician probably won't be able to offer a quick cure. Some parents, however, have been able to relieve (partially or completely) their colicky infants with an over-the-counter gas remedy for adults. Talk to your doctor about whether he or she thinks taking this medication would benefit your child. Here are a few other approaches to dealing with colic (or crying babies in general).

♦ Use the methods described in the "Crying" and "Coping with Crying" sections.

♦ If you're bottle-feeding the baby, try taking her off cow's milk. Some pediatricians feel that colic may be linked to a milk intolerance and suggest switching to a non–cow's milk formula.

♦ Hold the baby facing you, with his head over your shoulder and your shoulder pressing on his stomach.

♦ Hold the baby a little *less*. One school of thought maintains that some babies cry because their nervous systems aren't mature enough to handle the stimulation that comes with being held and stroked and talked to. But don't do this unless your physician advises you to.

♦ Put a hot water bottle on your knees, place the baby face down across it to warm his tummy, and stroke his back.

♦ Baby massage (see pages 59–60).

♦ Try swaddling. Being enveloped in a blanket may make the baby feel more comfortable.

♦ See the section on anger (pages 199–202).

believe are caused by hormonal shifts in a new mother's body, can last for hours or days, but in most cases they disappear within a few weeks. If you notice that your partner is experiencing any of these symptoms, there's not much you can do except be supportive. Encourage her to get out of the house for a while and see to it that she's eating healthily.

In a small number of cases, postpartum blues can develop into postpartum depression. According to the American College of Obstetricians and Gynecologists, postpartum depression, if not recognized and treated, may become worse or last longer than it needs to. Here are some symptoms to watch out for:

◆ Postpartum blues that don't go away after two weeks, or feelings of depression or anger that surface a month or two after the birth.
◆ Feelings of sadness, doubt, guilt, helplessness, or hopelessness that begin to disrupt your partner's normal functioning.
◆ Inability to sleep when tired, or sleeping most of the time, even when the baby is awake.
◆ Marked changes in appetite.
◆ Extreme concern and worry about the baby—or lack of interest in the baby and/or other members of the family.
◆ Fear of harming the baby or thoughts of self-harm.

Again, most of what your partner will go through after the birth is completely normal and nothing to worry about. If you're really concerned, however, encourage your partner to talk with you about what she's feeling and to see her doctor or a therapist.

Even Guys Get the Blues

Although postpartum blues or depression are almost always associated with women, the fact is that many men also get the blues after their babies are born. Men's blues, however, are not hormonally based like their partner's. The feelings of sadness, the mood swings, and the anxiety you may be experiencing are more likely the result of coming face to face with the reality of your changing life.

"The hearty congratulations at work last a few days," writes S. Adams Sullivan, author of *The Father's Almanac,* "but then your status as a celebrity wears off and you begin to notice that you're coming home every night to a demanding baby and a distraught wife, and the bills are piling up. . . . You look at your wife and . . . the healthy, radiant glow that made her beautiful while she was pregnant has disappeared, and you're tempted to agree with her when she gripes about her looks . . . you're getting maybe four and a half hours of sleep, total, and that's broken up into hour-and-a-half naps, so that you're nodding off every day at work and falling behind."

Fortunately, most men (and women, for that matter) don't suffer from any kind of postpartum depression. But if you do, you can take some comfort in knowing that it will eventually pass: you'll get caught up at work, the baby will settle into a routine, you'll get more sleep, and your wife's body will somehow get back to looking pretty much the way it did before she got pregnant.

Safety First

It may seem strange to talk about safety at a time when the baby is practically immobile and probably can't get into any serious trouble. But even at this age babies can do the most surprising things. Here are a few precautions you should take now to start making your home a little safer:

♦ Avoid beanbags. Most beanbag chairs and baby rests have been taken off the market, but there are still plenty of them in garages all over the country. There is more than a coincidental link between beanbags and suffocation deaths.

♦ Never leave the baby's car seat—with the baby in it, of course—balanced on anything. A flailing arm or leg, even a sneeze, might move the car seat enough for it to tip over.

♦ Put together a good first aid kit. You can find a list of items on page 140.

♦ Take an infant CPR class. Instruction is usually available at your local Red Cross or YMCA.

♦ Take a quick look at the safety measures described in later chapters (pages 138–41, for example). Start putting together the materials you'll need and get into the habit of doing such things as pointing pot handles toward the rear of the stove.

Notes:

First Smiles

What's Going On with the Baby

Physically

+ By the end of this month, most of your baby's innate reflexes will have disappeared. Sad but true. Nevertheless, she still holds her arms and legs away from her body, and there's plenty of twitching to go around.
+ Lying on her tummy, she can now hold her head at a 45-degree angle for a few minutes. And when she's sitting (a position she probably prefers by now), she's getting a lot better at keeping her head straight.
+ Your baby is now beginning to reach for objects. Grasping, which was once purely a reflex action, is now becoming voluntary. She even may be able to hold small objects for a few minutes at a time.
+ Although her vision is still limited to what's directly in front of her face, just about everything is now in focus. And because you're such an interesting sight, she'll follow you with her eyes everywhere you go.

Intellectually

+ As her brain develops, your baby will prefer more complex patterns. Instead of the simple, relatively motionless outline of your face, she now prefers your eyes and mouth, which are constantly changing shape.
+ If you touch her cheek now, she probably won't start sucking—an indication that she can now tell the difference between your finger and a milk-bearing nipple.
+ She is also now able to accommodate herself to various situations. If you're

holding her upright against your shoulder, she'll hold herself differently than if you're resting her on your knees.

♦ She gets excited when she sees familiar objects, but she has no sense of "object permanence" (which means that as far as the baby is concerned, anything she can't see simply doesn't exist).

Verbally

♦ Leaving behind the grunting and squeaking, your baby is adding to her repertoire some delightful cooing (a combination of a squeal and a gurgle), as well as some impressive oohs, ohhs, and ahhs.

♦ Crying, however, is still one of her favorite ways of communicating.

Emotionally/Socially

♦ And now, the moment you've been waiting for: your baby is finally able to smile at you (sorry, but until now those things you thought were smiles were probably just gas).

♦ As she becomes more and more interested in learning about her world (a process that hopefully won't stop for the rest of her life), your baby will really enjoy regular changes of scenery; she's also very capable of expressing excitement—and distress.

♦ She's awake about 10 hours a day; although she's stimulated more by touch than by social interaction, she'll stay awake longer if there are people around to amuse her.

What You're Going Through

Thinking about Sex

Most OB/GYNs advise their patients to refrain from intercourse for at least six weeks after giving birth. But before you mark that date on your calendar, re-member that the six-week rule is only a guideline. Resuming intercourse ulti-mately depends on the condition of your partner's cervix and vagina, and, more important, on how you're both feeling. Many couples begin having sex again in as little as three or four weeks, but it's not at all uncommon for couples to take as long as six months to fully reestablish their prepregnancy sex life.

Many factors—both physical and psychological—influence when and how a couple decides to resume their sex life. Here are a few:

♦ When you had sex with your partner before, she was the woman you loved. Now she's also a mother—a thought that may remind you of your own

Nonsexual and Almost Nonsexual Affection

Professors Phil and Carolyn Cowan have found that many couples need practice finding sensual ways to please each other short of intercourse. Hand-holding, back rubs, hair stroking while watching TV, or even gentle, nonsexual kissing are good for those times one of you isn't in the mood. If you're not in the mood but want to give—or receive— some nonsexual affection, tell your partner up front that there are no strings attached. Researchers have found that men and women who don't want sex are frequently afraid that the kiss or hug they need from, or want to give to, their partners will be misinterpreted as a sexual overture.

mother and can be a big turn-off. At the same time, in your new capacity as parent, you may remind your partner a little too much of her own father. She may also find it tough to reconcile her roles as lover and mother, and may see herself as unsexual.

♦ Your partner may not have fully recovered from her episiotomy or C-section.

♦ Your partner may be embarrassed if milk flows from her breasts when she's aroused.

♦ A lot of men find leaking breasts erotic. But if you don't—and she senses your feelings—she may worry that you don't find her desirable anymore.

♦ Some men have "emotional difficulty being sexual with the part of their wives that produced their children," says psychologist Jerrold Shapiro. And a lot of women find it difficult to think of their vaginas as sexual organs after seeing babies come out of them.

♦ You may resent your baby's unlimited access to your partner's breasts and feel that your partner is focusing more on the baby than on you.

♦ Your (or your partner's) motivation to have sex may have changed since your baby was born. If, for example, you or she were motivated to have sex because you really wanted to be a parent, sex after having a baby may feel a little anticlimactic, so to speak.

♦ Now that you have concrete proof (the baby) of your virility, you may feel more intimate with your partner than ever before.

When You and Your Partner are Out of Sync

Just as you and your partner can't always agree on what movie you want to see or what you want to have for dinner, you can't expect that you'll both feel sexually aroused at the same time. She might want to make love at a time when

The First Time . . . Again

When you do finally get around to making love, you should expect the first few times to be a period of tentative rediscovery for both of you. Her body has changed, and she may respond differently than she used to. Some studies have shown that after giving birth women experience a slightly decreased interest in vaginal stimulation and an increased interest in clitoral and breast stimulation. Also, women who experienced multiple orgasms before giving birth are less likely to do so, or will do so less frequently, now.

She may also be worried that having sex will hurt, and you may be afraid of the same thing or that those extra pounds she hasn't lost yet will interfere with her pleasure. Go slowly, take your cues from her, and give yourselves plenty of time to get used to each other again.

Sex researchers William Fisher and Janice Gray found that nursing mothers generally resume their sexual lives sooner than women who don't breastfeed. This is a little odd, considering that nursing mothers produce lower levels of ovarian hormones, which are responsible for producing vaginal lubrication. As a result, if your partner is nursing, her vagina may be much drier than before, making intercourse painful. Obviously, this doesn't mean she isn't aroused by you; it's simply a common postbirth condition. In situations like these, a little K-Y Jelly, Astroglide, or other over-the-counter lubricant will go a long way.

you're simply too tired to move. Or you might want to have sex when she's feeling "touched out," having spent an entire day with a baby crawling all over her, sucking her breasts.

The months right after the birth of a baby are a particularly vulnerable time for your sex life. "If you had a good sex life before and during the pregnancy, it is important to be intentional about keeping a positive sex life after the birth of your child," says Dr. William Stayton, a professor of human sexuality at the University of Pennsylvania. "If you did not have a good sex life before the pregnancy, then it is very likely that it will not get better after the birth of your child unless you intentionally give time and energy to your sexual relationship." Here are a few suggestions that might help smooth over some of the rough spots you'll invariably encounter:

♦ Figure out what, exactly, is motivating you to want to have sex. "Sex can be an expression of monogamy, intimacy, love, or even an affirmation of one's sexual identity ('I'm a man and this is what men do')," says Linda Perlin

Alperstein, an associate professor at the University of California, San Francisco. "It can also be the only way some of us ever get held and touched lovingly in our culture." And for some people (this is pretty rare, though) sex is thought of exclusively as a way to reproduce.

♦ Talk. "Unless the couple can talk about their sex life, their entire relationship may suffer, and that in turn will compound their sexual problems," write psychologists Libby and Arthur Colman.

♦ Negotiate. If you really want to have sex and she doesn't, ask her—without putting a lot of pressure on her—what, if anything, she'd be willing to do. Would she, for example, be willing to masturbate you? Would she hold you in her arms or let you touch her breasts while you stimulate yourself? It goes without saying (or at least it should) that you should be prepared to reciprocate. The object here is not to convince her to have sex with you; the two of you should be working toward creating an environment in which you both feel safe expressing your desires and in which each of you can turn the other down without fear of causing offense or hurting feelings.

♦ Be completely honest. If you and your partner agree that you'll hold each other like spoons and kiss, but that you won't touch each other's genitals, don't go over the line. Doing so will only make her tense and not trust you.

♦ Change your attitude. A lot of men have the idea that every erection has to be paired up with an ejaculation. "But the truth is that just being aroused can be nice—and quite enjoyable," says Linda Alperstein. "So rather than have no sexual life if you can't have the one you fantasize about, enjoy what you can have; just enjoy the fact that you can get aroused again. You don't have to actually reach an orgasm to experience pleasure."

♦ Take it easy. "While a positive sexual relationship is a very nice and important component of an enduring and happy marriage," writes psychologist Brad Sachs, "it will not, by itself, ensure one."

♦ Ask for—and give your partner—some nonsexual affection (see page 51).

Not Ready to Be a Father

One of the most consistent findings by researchers is that new fathers almost always feel unprepared for their new role. Personally, I would have been surprised if it were otherwise. As writer David L. Giveans says, "It is both unfair and unrealistic to expect a man . . . to automatically 'father' when his life experiences have skillfully isolated him from learning how."

When most of our fathers were raising us, a "good father" was synonymous with "good provider." He supported his family financially, mowed the lawn, washed the car, and maintained discipline in the home. No one seemed to care

"You're not real experienced at this father business, are you?"

whether he ever spent much time with his children; in fact, he was *discouraged* from doing so, and told to leave the kids to his wife, the "good mother."

Yesterday's "good father" has now retroactively become an emotionally distant, uncaring villain. And today's "good father," besides still being a breadwinner, is expected to be a real presence—physically and emotionally—in his kids' lives. This, in a nutshell, is exactly what most new fathers want. Most of us have no intention of being wait-till-your-father-comes-home dads and want to be more involved with our children than our own fathers were. The problem is that we just haven't had the training.

The solution? Quit complaining and jump right in. The "maternal instinct" that women are supposedly born with is actually acquired on the job. And that's exactly where you're going to develop your "paternal instinct."

Confusion

If there's one thing that set my first few months of fatherhood apart from the next few years, it was the confusing and often conflicting emotions I felt:

♦ On the one hand, I had a sense of incredible virility, power, and pride at having created a new life. On the other, I often felt helpless when I couldn't understand—let alone satisfy—the baby's needs.

♦ Most of the time I felt the most powerful kind of love for my tiny child. But sometimes I also felt ambivalent. And once in a while I felt a powerful anger—one that seemed to come out of nowhere—at the very same baby.

♦ Most of the time I felt particularly close to my wife—especially when we would admire our children together. But every so often I'd get suspicious that she loved them more than she did me.

Apparently I wasn't the only confused new dad around. "Almost all new fathers express some level of confusion," says psychologist Bruce Linton, who runs workshops for expectant and new fathers. But as if feeling confused isn't bad enough, Linton has found that new fathers "consistently express anxiety and concern that there's something wrong with them or that they're abnormal because they're confused."

Before you go off and check yourself into a mental hospital, there are a few things you should know. First, being confused isn't abnormal at all. After spending the day in Linton's workshop discussing their concerns with other men, new fathers are greatly relieved to find out that their feelings aren't all that different from those of any other new father. (And anyway, doesn't it seem logical that if almost everyone thinks he's abnormal, then being abnormal must really be the norm?) Second, this state of confusion—and the accompanying suspicions about your sanity—usually disappear by the end of the third month.

Fears—Lots of Them

The combination of feeling unprepared and confused at the same time can be rather frightening, and the first few months of fatherhood are riddled with fears. Here are some of the most common:

♦ Fear of not being able to live up to your own expectations.

♦ Fear of not being able to protect your children from physical harm as they grow and develop.

♦ Fear of not being able to deal with the most basic parenting responsibilities: feeding, clothing, earning enough money, dealing with the baby's illnesses.

♦ Fear of not being able to shield your child from some of the more abstract horrors of modern life: poverty, war, disease, the destruction of the environment . . .

♦ Fear of simply not being "ready" to assume the role of father.

♦ Fear of picking up the baby because you think you might hurt him.

♦ Fear of your anger at the baby.

Don't Panic

Taken together, the feelings of unpreparedness, the fears, and the confusion so many new fathers experience can be overwhelming. Unfortunately, some men respond to this turmoil by running away—emotionally, physically, or both—from their kids and their partners. If you're feeling unable to deal with your anxieties and your feelings, do *not* run. Find yourself a more experienced father about your age and ask him to help you sort things out (see pages 133–35 for information on fathers' groups). If you can't find another father, talk to your partner. And if none of those alternatives work, find a good therapist, preferably one with experience dealing with men's concerns. There *is* help out there; you just have to find it.

♦ Fear of not being able—or willing—to love the baby enough.
♦ Fear of not being in control (see pages 73–74).
♦ Fear of repeating the mistakes made by your own father (see pages 71–72).
♦ Fear that if you discuss your fears with your partner, she'll misinterpret them and think you don't love her or the baby.

Some fears—such as fear of poverty and war, or of not being ready—you just can't do anything about. But others you can. For example, fear of not being able to handle the little things can be overcome by practice; fear of hurting the baby can also be overcome by spending more time carrying, stroking, picking up, and holding him—babies are not nearly as fragile as they look; and the fear of discussing things with your partner can be cured (to a certain extent) by taking a deep breath and telling her what you feel. She's going through many of the same things you are and will be relieved to find that she's not alone. Guaranteed.

Whatever your fears, you need to start by admitting to yourself that they exist and remembering that all new fathers are afraid sometimes. In his book *Fatherjournal*, David Steinberg eloquently describes coming to terms with himself and his fears. "I was going to be the perfect father: loving, caring, nurturing, soft. . . . I was going to do it right. . . . Tonight I see how scared I am. There is so much to do for this little creature who screams and wriggles and needs and doesn't know what he needs and relies on me to figure it out. . . . I need to accept my fear, my reluctance, my instinct to flee. I have to start from where I am instead of where the model new-age father would be."

Rethinking What It Means to Be a Man

There are two major reasons why so many of us would prefer to drive ten miles down the wrong road rather than stop and ask for directions. First, from the time we were little boys, we've been socialized to associate knowledge with masculinity—in other words, real men know everything, so admitting to being lost is a sign of weakness (and, of course, a lack of masculinity). Second, and even worse, we've also been socialized to be strong, independent, and goal-oriented, so asking for help is a sign of weakness (and, again, a lack of masculinity).

Nothing in the world can bring these two factors into play faster than the birth of a baby. Because of the near-total absence of active, involved, nurturing male role models, most new fathers can't seriously claim that they know what to do with a new baby (although never having cooked before didn't prevent my father from insisting he could make the best blueberry pancakes we'd ever taste; boy, was he wrong).

Getting help seems like the obvious solution to the ignorance problem, but most men don't want to seem helpless or expose their lack of knowledge by asking anyone. Now toss in a few more ingredients:

+ The confusion and fears we've been feeling lately.
+ The prevailing attitude that a man who is actively involved with his children—especially if he's the primary caretaker—is not as masculine as his less-involved brothers.
+ Psychologist Henry Biller's observation that "too many men get caught up in the idea that to be an effective parent they must adopt a more maternal or mothering role."

It's easy to see how the whole experience of becoming a father can lead so many new fathers to wonder secretly (no one would ever *openly* admit to having these thoughts) whether or not they've retained their masculinity. All too often the result of this kind of thinking is that fathers leave all the child-rearing to their partners and thereby leave their kids essentially without a father. As Biller writes, "Children are at a particular disadvantage when they are deprived of constructive experiences with their fathers. Infants and young children are unlikely to be provided with other opportunities to form a relationship with a caring and readily available adult male if their father is not emotionally committed to them."

So you have a choice. Either accept the hardest yet most rewarding challenge you'll probably ever face by becoming an actively involved father and taking on a significant share of the responsibility for raising your children, or take the easy way out and leave it all to someone else. What would a "real" man do?

You and Your Baby

Awakening the Senses

Your baby was born equipped with the same five basic senses you were. And although his senses would probably develop pretty well without any additional help, there's a lot you can do (while having fun at the same time) to encourage development by exposing him to a broad range of sensory stimulation.

TASTE

By putting drops of various foods (in liquid) on babies' tongues, researchers have proven that babies have definite likes and dislikes. You're not going to try this, of course. At this age, your baby has no business eating anything but breast milk or formula. Save the experiments with real taste sensations for when you wean your baby (see pages 205–7). In the meantime, give the baby lots of different objects to put in his mouth. But be extremely careful that none of them is small enough to be a choking hazard or has removable pieces or sharp edges.

SMELL

Offer the baby a wide variety of things to smell:
- If you're cooking, let her smell the spices and other ingredients.
- If you're out for a walk, let her smell the flowers.
- Try some experiments to see whether she prefers sweet smells to sour ones.
- Be careful, though. Make sure she doesn't get any of these things in her mouth, and don't experiment with extremely strong smells. Also, stay away from ammonia, bleach, gasoline, paint thinner, pool or garden chemicals, and any other toxic materials you may have around the house.

SIGHT

- Experiment with the baby's sight. Regularly change the patterns and keep track of which ones he prefers. Over the course of the next few months he'll advance from simple shapes and patterns to more complex ones.
- Show him mirrors, pictures, and photographs.
- Take the baby out for a walk and let him see what's going on in the world.

TOUCH

Expose the baby to as many textures as possible: the satin edges of his blanket; the plastic (or cloth) on his diaper; the family dog; a window; your computer keyboard. Let the baby feel each object for as long as he's interested. And don't

> ## No Baby Talk, Please
> Whenever you talk to your baby, pay close attention to your voice. Your natural, conversational voice is best because it exposes the baby to English as it is actually spoken. For some reason I've never been able to understand, many people can't bring themselves to speak naturally to a baby. Instead, they smile the biggest fake smile they can and say things like "Cootchie-cootchie widduw baby-poo, can I pinchy-winchy your cheeky-weeky?" Is that really the way you want your baby to learn how to speak? Need I say more?

limit yourself to the baby's hands; you can gently rub objects on the baby's cheeks, arms, or legs. (From a very young age, both my daughters loved me to rub the bottoms of their feet on my two-day beard growth.) Again, use common sense here. Be gentle and don't leave any objects with the baby.

HEARING

♦ Expose the baby to as wide a variety of sounds as possible: the radio; any musical instruments you have around the house; construction sites (if they're not too loud). Does your baby seem to prefer one kind of noise—or music—over another?

♦ For fun, take a small bell, hold it behind the baby, and ring it gently. Does he try to turn around? Now move the bell to one side. Did the baby notice the change?

♦ Don't forget about your own voice. Make sounds, changing the pitch of your voice; sing; and even have leisurely chats (okay, monologues) with the baby.

♦ Play imitation games. Make a noise (a Bronx cheer is always a good place to start) and see whether the baby responds. It may take a few minutes or even a few days to get a reply. Once you do, try the same noise a few more times and then switch roles, having the baby initiate the "conversation" so you can imitate her.

Baby Massage

Many parents in Africa, Asia, and India massage their babies every day. But in the United States this idea is just catching on. And in the eyes of some, it's about time. According to researcher Tiffany Field, massage:

♦ Facilitates the parent-infant bonding process and the development of warm, positive relationships.

> **Massage for Preemies**
>
> Over a dozen researchers have seriously explored the question of whether baby massage could help preterm infants. One study found that preemies who had daily ten-minute sessions of neck, shoulder, back, and leg massage, and five minutes a day of gentle limb flexing gained 47 percent more weight than preterm babies who got no massage, even though the two groups did not differ in calorie intake. In addition, massaged infants were awake and active a greater percentage of the time, developed more quickly, and required six fewer days of hospitalization.

♦ Reduces stressful responses to painful procedures like vaccines (at least for the baby).

♦ Reduces pain associated with teething and constipation.

♦ Reduces colic.

♦ Helps induce sleep.

♦ Makes parents feel good while they're massaging their infants.

Sounds like it's at least worth a try, doesn't it? Here's how to do it:

1. With your fingertips, gently massage the baby's forehead, nose, and mouth.
2. Starting in the middle of your baby's chest, use a flat hand to stroke outward.
3. Do the same thing on his back—start from the middle and stroke outward.
4. Take one of the baby's feet with one hand. With the other, hold the baby's ankle like a baseball bat and slide your hand toward the thigh. Repeat with the other foot.
5. Do the same thing for the arms: start at the wrist and move toward the shoulder.

The best time to massage is when the baby is calm. You might want to rub a little baby oil or lotion on your hands before you start, and be sure to use a combination of straight and circular strokes.

It's especially important to keep the pressure gentle yet firm. Babies respond negatively to a very light touch, which they perceive as tickling. If at all possible, try to do some massage every day (or split the duties with your partner). If you're interested in learning more about baby massage, several books on the subject are probably available at your local library. One of the best is Vimala McClure's *Infant Massage: A Handbook for Loving Parents.*

The Importance of Squirming Around

Most two-month-old babies are not really mobile. They can raise their heads about 45 degrees, but rolling over is still a ways away. Nevertheless, it's a good idea to let your baby exercise her muscles. Here are a few ways to do this:

♦ Stop swaddling (if you haven't already). Your baby needs to practice using her arms and hands, something she won't be able to do if she's all bundled up in a blanket.

♦ When putting the baby down, alternate among front, back, left side, and right side. This encourages the baby to use as many different muscles as possible. Babies who spend all day on one side (including front or back) generally don't learn to lift their heads as quickly as those who are shifted from side to side.

Introducing the Doctor

If you went to all your partner's prenatal doctor visits, the schedule of visits to your baby's pediatrician will seem quite leisurely—only eight (usually called well-baby checkups) the entire first year. Whether or not you got into

Vaccinations

There has been a lot of controversy lately about vaccinations (Are the vaccines themselves dangerous? Are the risks worth the rewards?), and a small but growing number of people are electing not to have their children inoculated. On pages 62–65 you'll find a chart listing the vaccines, the possible side effects, and what might happen to someone who's not inoculated. If you're thinking of skipping the vaccinations, keep these points in mind:

♦ Almost all public schools, and many private ones, require proof of vaccination before admitting a child.

♦ Not vaccinating your kids can be a viable option only if everyone else's kids *are* vaccinated, thus reducing the chance that your child will be exposed to health risks. This is known as "herd immunity": if enough people are immune, they'll protect the rest of the "herd." Imagine what would happen if everyone decided not to vaccinate.

VACCINE	RISKS (👎) / REWARDS (👍)
Diphtheria, Pertussis, Tetanus (DPT) or Diphtheria, Tetanus (DT) or DTaP: same as above, minus pertussis part for babies who have: ♦ history of seizures ♦ suspected or known neuro- logical disease ♦ reactions to previous shot	👍 almost all protected after 3 doses plus booster 👎 you'll need to observe baby care- fully for 72 hours after shot 👎 some fussiness, drowsiness, sore- ness, or a lump at injection site 👎 fever for 24 hours after the shot is common 👎 irritation of the brain occurs in 1 in 100,000 kids, and rarely (1 in 310,000), permanent brain damage results. *Note:* Most of the risks are associ- ated with the pertussis component. The only risk associated with the diphtheria and tetanus parts is local (injection site swelling)
Hepatitis B: a noninfectious vaccine produced from cultures	👍 almost all children protected after 3 doses 👎 no adverse reactions, but occa- sional fussiness 👎 possible soreness at injection site, low-grade fever, or headache
Haemophilus (HiB)	👍 90–100 percent protection rate after the full series of shots 👎 soreness and/or lump at the injection site 👎 fever (rarely above 101 degrees) for 12–24 hours after shot
Measles	👍 over 95 percent protected after one dose 👎 10–20 percent have mild fever or rash 10 days after shot 👎 1 in 1,000,000 may develop a brain disorder

WHAT IT PREVENTS	RISKS IF YOU GET THE DISEASE
Diphtheria	♦ extremely contagious
	♦ attacks the throat and nose, interferes with breathing, and causes paralysis
	♦ damages heart, kidneys, nerves
	♦ 10–35 percent death rate
Pertussis (whooping cough): prior to the invention of this vaccine, pertussis caused as many deaths as all other contagious diseases combined	♦ can cause brain damage, pneumonia, and seizures
	♦ can cause death (1–2 percent)
	♦ most severe in young babies
Tetanus (lockjaw), caused by dirt getting in cuts	♦ causes painful muscle contractions
	♦ 20–60 percent of kids die
Hepatitis B	♦ important cause of viral hepatitis
	♦ complications include cirrhosis, chronic active hepatitis, and liver cancer
Haemophilus Influenza type B, bacterial infection of children under 5	♦ causes 12,000 cases of meningitis and 8,000 cases of deep-seated infections (bones, joint, heart, lungs, throat) each year
	♦ 5 percent mortality rate
Measles	♦ a most serious, common childhood disease
	♦ high fever (103–105 degrees) and rash for up to 10 days
	♦ may cause pneumonia or ear infection
	♦ 1 in 100 kids becomes deaf or develops brain disorders

(continued on next page)

(continued from pages 62–63)

VACCINE	RISKS (👎) / REWARDS (👍)
Mumps	👍 99 percent protected after one dose 👎 rare fever, rashes, and swelling of glands after vaccination
Rubella	👍 over 95 percent protected after one dose 👍 getting it now protects future fetuses of girl babies 👍 children of pregnant women can be vaccinated without risk to mother 👎 1 percent of young children will have temporary leg, arm, joint pain
MMR measles, mumps, rubella vaccines	👍 protection is as good as when vaccines are given separately 👍 side effects are same as when given separately
Oral Polio (OPV): three kinds of polio virus—your child needs all 3 vaccines to be protected	👍 drops, not shots 👍 95 percent receiving all 3 doses are protected 👍 no common reactions 👎 1 in 4 million chance of paralysis 👎 1 in 12 million chance of actually getting polio

the doctor-visit habit before the baby was born, make every effort to go to as many well-baby visits (and not-so-well-baby visits) as you can. Your doing so is good for everyone, says James Levine, head of the Fatherhood Project at the Families and Work Institute.

♦ Your baby will know that he can turn to you for help and that you'll be there to comfort him when he needs it.

♦ Your doctor will be able to get some of *your* family history to apply to the

WHAT IT PREVENTS	RISKS IF YOU GET THE DISEASE
Mumps	◆ causes fever and swelling of salivary glands ◆ may cause irritation of heart, pancreas, or thyroid ◆ can cause permanent deafness and temporary brain disorder
Rubella (German measles)	◆ can cause birth defects in fetus of pregnant women ◆ symptoms are mild, often missed
Mumps, Measles, Rubella	
Polio	◆ causes paralysis of arms and legs ◆ interferes with breathing ◆ 1 in 10 kids with polio dies

baby. And since most of what pediatricians know about their young patients comes from what the parents tell them, your input doubles the amount of information the doctor can use to make a diagnosis.

◆ You'll be more in touch with your child and more involved in his life.

Most doctor visits will be pretty much the same: the nurse will try to convince the baby to lie flat enough to be measured, and to sit still on a scale long enough to get weighed. Then the doctor will poke the baby's stomach, measure his head, and ask you a series of questions about the baby's health. The big events at most doctor visits for the first several years are the vaccinations.

We'll discuss some specific medical questions in later chapters. But for now, here's a fairly typical schedule of well-baby checkups and the vaccinations your baby will receive at each visit:

AGE AT TIME OF VISIT	VACCINATION(S) GIVEN
birth–2 weeks	Hepatitis B
2 months	DPT and Hepatitis B
3 months	OPV and Haemophilus Influenza B
4 months	DPT and Hepatitis B
5 months	OPV and Haemophilus Influenza B
6 months	DPT and Hepatitis B
8 months	OPV and Haemophilus Influenza B
12 months	MMR and TB test

Notes:

Let the Games Begin

What's Going On with the Baby

Physically

♦ As more and more of his reflexes disappear, your baby's body is changing. He can now keep his hands open (instead of balled up in tiny fists), and when you put him down on his tummy, he extends his legs instead of automatically rolling up into a little ball like a pill bug.

♦ But he can't yet tell one side of his body from the other, and he moves both legs or both arms together.

♦ When you pull him from a reclining position, he'll try to stand up, pressing his feet against whatever he was lying on.

♦ His head is bobbing around a lot less, and if you can get him into a sitting position, he can probably sit fairly well for a few seconds (he'll still need plenty of support). He may also be able to clap his hands.

♦ Your baby is getting much better at grasping things—a development some experts feel is a new reflex, designed to develop your baby's hand-eye coordination. "Everything that the child grasps is brought to the eyes and everything he sees evokes an effort to grasp," says Dr. Wolff.

Intellectually

♦ Moving objects are a source of nearly endless fascination. Your baby will follow with his eyes and head an object moving from one side of his head to the other.

♦ One day your baby will catch sight of his own hand on its way into his mouth. Until this very moment, he had no idea that the thing he's been sucking on for the past few months actually belongs to him. Best of all, he now realizes that objects (or at least his hand) can exist for at least two reasons at the same time: to look at *and* to suck on.

♦ As a result of this startling, and incredibly important, revelation, your baby will spend as much as 15 minutes at a stretch intently staring at his squiggling fingers and then shoving them into his mouth. He'll repeat the process over and over and over.

♦ The baby is now able to tell the difference between various objects; he prefers circular shapes to stripes.

♦ He is also able to make associations between certain objects and qualities linked to them. For example, he may associate your partner with food and you with play, and will react differently to each of you.

Verbally

♦ Although most of your baby's vocalizing is crying, he's making some delightful, soothing, single-syllable sounds.

♦ He's now beginning to use his vocalizing for a purpose—if you listen carefully, you should be able to tell the difference between his "I'm hungry," "I'm tired," and "Change my diaper" cries.

♦ He's now also attentively listening to all the sounds around him and distinguishes speech from any other sound.

Emotionally/Socially

♦ At this point your baby's schedule of eating, sleeping, diaper filling, and being alert is fairly regular.

♦ When it comes to people, he has strong likes and dislikes, crying or calming down depending on who holds him. He'll also smile at familiar people, stare at strangers.

♦ He'll stare, absorbed with his surroundings, for up to 30 minutes at a time.

What You're Going Through

Worried about SIDS

Every year seven thousand children die of SIDS (Sudden Infant Death Syndrome). Striking one out of every thousand babies, it is the most common cause of death of children between one week and one year old.

Although government and private agencies spend millions of dollars each year in the fight against SIDS, scientists have been unable to figure out what, exactly, causes the disease. And there's no medical test to determine which babies are at the greatest risk. Here is what scientists *do* know:

♦ SIDS is most likely to strike infants two to four months old.

♦ Ninety percent of deaths happen by six months, but SIDS still strikes children up to one year old.

♦ It is more likely to occur to boys than girls, to preterm babies, to multiple-birth babies, and to babies from families in which a parent or caretaker smokes or bottle-feeds.

♦ The disease is more common in cold weather, when respiratory infections and overheating are more common. Both have been linked to SIDS.

Although two-thirds of all SIDS babies have no risk factors, there are a few things you can do to minimize the risk:

♦ Make sure your baby sleeps on his back. When my older daughter was born in 1990, the then-current wisdom was that babies should not sleep on their backs because of the risk of choking if the baby spit up. But by the time my second was born in 1993, the spit-up theory had been debunked. If your baby has been sleeping on his stomach, it's not too late to change (sure, he's been doing it all his life, but still, it's been only three months). After four months, making the stomach-to-back shift is far less critical.

♦ Don't smoke and don't let anyone else smoke near the baby.

♦ Don't overdress the baby (see the section on dressing, pages 79–80).

♦ Have your baby sleep on a firm mattress: no pillows, fluffy blankets, cushiony sofas, waterbeds, thick rugs, or beanbags. Make sure the mattress fits snugly into the crib so that the baby can't slip between the mattress and the crib frame. And take out of the crib all the plush animals, extra blankets, and other things that might accidentally cover the baby.

♦ Breastfeed.

♦ Don't panic. Although SIDS is a horrible, devastating experience for any parent, remember that 999 out of 1,000 babies *don't* die of it.

What to Do If You Lose Your Baby to SIDS

The loss of a child is a terrible thing, something that will affect you and your partner for the rest of your lives. Too often SIDS affects couples who haven't been together very long, and the strain can be especially taxing to their new relationship. But no matter how long a couple has been together, the loss of a child will have a devastating effect on their relationship.

"Surviving grief does not mean escaping from it," says Amy Hillyard

Grief: Not for Women Only

For better or worse, men and women are socially and culturally conditioned to behave in certain ways in certain situations. We could spend a lot of time arguing about the advantages and disadvantages of our socialization, but one thing we can all agree on is that men, generally, aren't allowed to experience or express grief in a way that is healthy to themselves or to those who love them.

Women are more likely to talk about their grief—they have more intimate friends and are more willing to ask for help. They're also more likely to get offered help. Men, however, are less likely to talk about their grief, preferring to internalize it and remain silent. They have fewer intimate friends and avoid asking for help. They also get offered a lot less help.

Men have some very specific needs when it comes to grieving. Here are some wonderful suggestions from the SIDS Alliance in Baltimore:

♦ Talk to your family—especially your wife. "Grief is the stone that bears one down, but two bear it lightly," said William Hauff in the nineteenth century. Let people know you're doing as much as you can and let them know how they can help you.

♦ Have quality "alone" time. You need time to sort through all

Jensen, author of *Healing Grief*. "Grief itself is the healing process and you must go through it. Grief will change you, but you have some control over whether the changes are for better or for worse."

Marion McNurlen of the Minnesota SIDS Alliance suggests that grieving couples do as many of the following as possible:

♦ Don't assume the other doesn't know what you're feeling or what you're going through.

♦ Schedule some time to talk to each other. You and your partner have experienced the same physical loss, but you won't grieve at the same pace, or at the same time. You need to check in with each other often.

♦ Have other people to talk to. Your partner can't be there for you (nor you for her) all the time. Call your friends, clergy person, or therapist.

♦ Touch each other. Often, the completely normal feelings of blame (either of yourself or of your partner) lead to not wanting to touch or be touched. At the same time, though, you and your partner may be nearly screaming inwardly for the other's touch, but you're afraid to ask, afraid of burdening the questions running through your brain. Think about keeping a journal.

♦ Decrease your social activities. Many men seek out new hobbies or other activities, but these only detract from the grieving you really need to do.

♦ Cry. It's just about the hardest thing to do for most of us, but don't try to keep down that lump in your throat or swallow your tears. Crying releases some tension and can actually make you feel better.

♦ Get angry. Anger is a natural part of the grieving process and holding it back or ignoring it won't make it disappear. There's nothing wrong with being angry; it's what you do with the feeling that counts, so find a way to express your anger that won't hurt others. Exercise is perhaps the best outlet for it.

♦ Find a support system. For many men, asking for help is even tougher than crying. But research has shown that what men find most helpful is a caring listener, someone patient, someone, perhaps, who is going through (or has recently gone through) the same experience. Local hospitals are an excellent source of referrals to support groups. So is the SIDS Alliance, which has counselors available twenty-four hours a day. You can reach them at (800) 221-SIDS (7437).

the other with your own needs. Physical closeness may be more important now than at any other time in your relationship.

♦ Try to have some fun. "It is common for grieving parents to have a strong sense that it is disrespectful of their child for them to laugh," says McNurlen. "But laughter is very healing, you can deeply miss your child and have fun once in a while."

Examining Your Relationship with Your Father

As you continue to grow and develop as a father, you may find yourself spending a lot of time thinking about your own father. Was he the kind of father you'd like to use as a role model, or was he exactly the kind of father you don't want to be? Was he supportive and nurturing, or was he absent or abusive? Like it or not, it is the relationship you had with your father when you were young that sets the tone for your relationship with your own children.

Depending on your perspective, this is either good news or bad news. If you are satisfied with your relationship with your dad and you'd like to be the kind

Well, Dad, I'll tell you: Every time I face a dilemma about parenting, I ask myself, "What would Dad do?"...And then I do the opposite.

SIPRESS

of father he was, you don't have much to worry about. "A cohesive boyhood home atmosphere in which the father and mother worked together," writes researcher John Snarey, "predicts that the boy who grew up in it will provide more care for his own children's social-emotional development in adolescence."

But if your relationship with your father was not everything it should have been, you may be afraid that you are somehow destined to repeat your father's mistakes. And you may have started to act accordingly. Psychologist Bruce Linton has observed that if a man's father was abusive, he may begin to withdraw or disengage from parenting his own infant out of "an unconscious or conscious desire to protect his child from his own fear of being abusive." And when the son of an absent father becomes a father himself, says Linton, "He often carries a deep grief or longing for the father he never had, and this feeling is activated as he experiences his own infant."

If you're finding yourself doing—or not doing—things with your baby out of fear, you can relax. At least a little. Dr. Snarey found that new fathers seem to take the good from their fathers and throw away the bad. In fact, many new fathers are able to turn to their advantage the example of a less-than-perfect relationship with their fathers. Here are some common scenarios:

♦ Men whose fathers were distant or non-nurturant often provide high levels of care for their children's social-emotional and intellectual-academic development in adolescence.

◆ Men whose fathers provided inconsistent or inadequate supervision tend to provide high levels of care for their children's physical-athletic development in childhood.

◆ Men whose fathers used or threatened to use physical punishment that instilled fear in them as boys generally provide high levels of care for their own children's physical-athletic development in childhood.

Taking On More Responsibility

Nearly two-thirds of the men in Dr. Bruce Drobeck's research studies stated that the biggest change in their lives since they became fathers was that they had taken on more responsibility. Drobeck doesn't say where "taking on more responsibility" ranked for the remaining third, but I can't imagine any new father not experiencing at least *some* increase. Then again, it depends on how one defines the term.

If you think, for example, that "taking on more responsibility" means only that you are spending the same amount of time on child care as your partner, you may not view those two extra dinners you plan and prepare or the three extra loads of laundry you now do each week as an increase. But I do. One new father, a man who had been out of work for four years, became more responsible when he started looking more realistically at his employment situation. "I just have to lower my sights," he said. "I can't hold out for the exact position I want." Sounds quite responsible to me.

Whatever definition of responsibility you settle on, you'll undoubtedly find that you're focusing much more on your family now, and you're spending more time thinking about the consequences of your actions. "A D.W.I. would put a hardship on the family," said one new father who quit having a few drinks before driving home from the golf course.

For me, being more responsible meant obeying the speed limits (or trying to) and not accelerating at yellow traffic lights. For you, however, it might mean anything from giving up bungee jumping or alligator wrestling to reducing the aggressiveness of your investments.

So whether you call it "taking on more responsibility," "changing your priorities," or "putting your family first," these completely normal behavioral changes all have at least one thing in common. Each, in Bruce Drobeck's words, gives the new father "a positive motivation for personal improvement and growth."

Losing Your Grip

"The baby cries, the parent answers," writes Ellen Galinsky. "The baby is hungry, the parent provides food. The baby is awake most of the night, so is the parent. Parents feel as if their old life, their ability to plan, to have a reliable pattern to their days, is slipping away. . . . They don't know how to gauge themselves. The chores, the repetitious cycles of feeding, changing, putting the baby to sleep, seem endless. Night blurs into day. Time and their ability to control it, even count on it, seem far beyond their grasp, perhaps forever." Sounds like a horror story, doesn't it?

Of course, no one wants to lose control. But the feeling of losing one's grip on one's own life is particularly hard for men. Although there aren't any guaranteed cures for feeling out of control, there are two deceptively simple things you can do to at least take the edge off the feeling:

- ♦ Sit down with your partner and schedule some regular breaks for each of you: from the baby, from each other, from the house. You'll be amazed at how rejuvenated you'll feel after even just a couple of hours alone, doing something non-baby-related. This isn't a one-shot deal—try to schedule breaks once a week or more often, if you need to.
- ♦ Learn to accept that some things are within your control and that some things aren't. Babies—at least at this age—aren't.

You and Your Baby

Let the Games Begin

Playing with your baby is one of the most important things you can do for him. Researchers have found that early parent-child play can speed up the attachment process. In addition, kids who are played with a lot as babies are more attentive and interactive as they grow up, and end up with higher self-esteem than kids who weren't played with as much.

But before you mount that basketball hoop, remember that at this stage of life babies have literally just discovered themselves, and watching and experimenting with their own little bodies are quite enough to keep them occupied for a big chunk of their waking time.

At this age, the first "game" you play with your baby starts off with nothing more than his giving you a smile. If you respond nicely, he'll smile at you again. After repeating this a few times (it may even take a few days), your baby will learn that what *he* does can lead to a response from *you*. That seemingly simple realization is the basis for any kind of meaningful interaction your baby will have with other people.

Nuts and Bolts

For now, most babies have no idea what to do with rattles, keys, or anything else that needs to be grabbed. This doesn't mean, however, that you shouldn't make regular attempts to introduce some objects into the baby's life. Just don't take it personally if your gesture is completely ignored.

You don't really need any more equipment or supplies than last month. However, you might want to hang a few more pictures of faces where the baby can see them easily. Also, be sure to review the "Awakening the Senses" section, pages 58–59.

A fun experiment: tie one end of a ribbon loosely to the baby's ankle and the other to a mobile. Make the ribbon taut enough so that if the baby moves his leg, he'll also move the mobile. After a few minutes, most (but definitely not all) babies at this age will begin to see a cause and effect relationship developing and will begin to move the tied leg more than the other. Move the ribbon to the other leg, then to the arms, and see how well the baby adapts. A note of caution: never leave the room—even for a minute—with the baby tied to the mobile.

Music

While it's way too early to introduce your baby to music in any serious way, it's not too early to acclimate him. And if you pay attention, you'll notice that he already has a rudimentary sense of rhythm. Lay him on the floor and turn on the stereo (not too loud, please). Notice how he moves his arms and legs rhythmically—not in *time* to the music, but definitely in *response* to it. Try different types of music. Do his movements change as you change the style?

Here are a few things to keep in mind as you're thinking about introducing your baby to music:

♦ Kids are surrounded by language from their first days (in fact, there's plenty of research showing that kids respond to linguistic rhythms and patterns they heard even before they were born).

♦ Kids learn music in much the same way as they do language: they start off by listening and absorbing. And remember: "It is not possible to harm a child by allowing her to listen to too much music," says music education researcher Edwin Gordon.

♦ Play a wide variety of music. Major or minor keys, fast or slow tempos, simple or complex rhythms, and the types of instruments are not important at this stage.

♦ Select music you like too (after all, you'll be listening as well).

♦ Some babies this age may try to imitate tones they hear. This is, however, extremely rare.

Reading: From Birth through Eight Months

Feeling a little silly about the prospect of sitting down and reading to your baby? Consider this: "When children have been read to, they enter school with larger vocabularies, longer attention spans, greater understanding of books and print, and consequently have the fewest difficulties in learning to read," writes Jim Trelease, author of *The New Read Aloud Handbook*. And in 1985, a U.S. Department of Education report stated, "The single most important activity for building the knowledge required for eventual success in reading is reading aloud to children."

Still not convinced? How about this: 60 percent of prison inmates are illiterate, 85 percent of juvenile offenders have reading problems, and 44 percent of adult Americans do not read a *single* book in the course of a year. Clearly, reading is an important habit to develop, and it's never too early to start.

What to Read When

For the first few months of your baby's life, your reading probably won't seem to be having much effect on him. Sometimes he'll stare at the book, sometimes not. Once in a while a flailing arm might hit the book, but it's completely accidental. It doesn't really matter what you read at this stage, just as long as you do it. It's a great opportunity for you and the baby to snuggle together and for him to get to know the rhythm and feel of our language.

At about three months, your baby may start holding your finger while you read to him. While it doesn't seem like much, this tiny gesture is a clear indication that he's starting to become aware of the book as a separate object and that he likes what you're doing. Look for books with simple, uncluttered drawings as well as poetry and nursery rhymes.

At four months, your baby will sit still and listen attentively while you're reading. He may even reach out to scratch the pages of the book. Don't get too excited, though, he's a while away from being able to identify anything on the page. Nursery rhymes, finger plays (this little piggy went to market and so on), and books with pictures of other babies are big hits at this stage.

At about five months most babies are just starting to respond to your pointing. There are two ways to take advantage of this new development: first, watch your baby's eyes, then point to and talk about what he is already focusing on. Second, point to something and encourage the infant to look where you're pointing.

At six months babies will respond to what you're reading by bouncing up and down or chuckling before you get to a familiar part of the story. If you've been reading regularly to your baby for a few months, you may notice that he has developed clear preferences for books and will let you know which one he wants you to read. A word of warning: at this age babies have an irresistible need to put everything into their mouths, and books are no exception. But first they'll want to scratch, tear, pat, rub, hit, and get into a serious tug-of-war with you over the book. To avoid these problems before they start, give your baby something else to put in his mouth while you're reading to him, and try to distract him with noise books (the cow says "moo," the airplane goes "whooosh").

At about seven months your baby's grabbing and tearing are now slightly more purposeful, and you may notice an occasional attempt to turn pages. It will be another month or two, though, until he's actually able to do so. Plot is pretty well wasted on babies this age. But he'll like books with brightly colored pictures of familiar objects, as well as those that encourage you to make different sounds.

READY, SET . . .

Here are a few things to keep in mind when you're getting ready to read:

- Select a regular place for reading.
- Set aside a regular time, when you will be able to devote your full attention to the baby and the book. Just before or just after a nap is usually good.
- Try to read for at least fifteen minutes each day. Be prepared: you may have to do this in several installments. Kids' attention spans average only about three minutes at this age, but vary widely (my older daughter would sit in my lap for an hour at a time, whereas my younger couldn't sit still for more than three seconds).
- Reading to your child is for *her*, not for you. So if she arches her back, squirms, lurches forward, or does anything to let you know she's not happy, stop immediately—you're wasting your time. If you don't, the baby will begin to associate reading with discomfort.
- Don't read things that are developmentally inappropriate. "The difference between whether kids enjoyed it or not," say researchers Linda Lamme and Athol Packer, "was whether or not the parents adjusted their bookreading behavior to the developmental levels of their infants."

A list of appropriate titles follows. This is by no means a definitive list. With about five thousand new children's titles published each year, the pool of good books never stops growing. I strongly urge you to get to know your local

librarians, who are always up to date, or to subscribe to *Children's Literature,*
a wonderful newsletter that reviews current children's books (the address is
in the resource guide at the end of the book).

. . . GO!

GENERAL INTEREST FOR THE FIRST SIX TO EIGHT MONTHS
Baby Animal Friends, Phoebe Dunn (board book)
The Baby (and others), John Burningham
Baby Farm Animals, Garth Williams
Baby's Book of Babies, Kathy Henderson
Baby's First Words, Lars Wik
Baby's First Year, Phyllis Hoffman
Baby's Home, Tana Hoban
First Things First, Charlotte Voake
Hand Rhymes, Marc Brown
Happy Baby, Angie and Sage
I See (and others), Rachel Isadora
Pat the Bunny, Dorothy Kunhardt
Pat the Cat, Edith Kunhardt
Peek-a-Boo!, Janet and Allan Ahlberg
Spot's Toys, Eric Hill
This Is Me, Lenore Blegvad (board book)
Ten Little Babies, Debbie MacKinnon (board book)
Trot Trot to Boston: Play Rhymes for Baby
Welcome, Little Baby (and others), Aliki
What Do Babies Do? Debby Slier (board book)
What Is It? Tana Hoban (board book)

MOTHER GOOSE, LULLABIES, POETRY AND SONGS,
FINGERPLAYS
These are great for kids of all ages. Start now and return to them as often as
you like.
The Baby's Bedtime Book, Kay Chorao
A First Caldecott Collection: The House That Jack Built and *A Frog He*
   Would A-Wooing Go
A Second Caldecott Collection: Sing a Song of Sixpence and *Three Jovial*
   Huntsmen
A Third Caldecott Collection: Queen of Hearts and *The Farmer's Boy*
The House that Jack Built, Janet Stevens

The Mother Goose Treasury, Raymond Briggs
Old Mother Hubbard, Alice and Martin Provensen
The Random House Book of Mother Goose, Arnold Lobel
Read-Aloud Rhymes for the Very Young, selected by Jack Prelutsky
Ring a Ring O-Roses, Flint Public Library
Sing a Song of Popcorn: Every Child's Book Of Poems, selected by
    Beatrice S. De Regniers et al.
The Complete Story of the Three Blind Mice, John Ivimey
Three Little Kittens, Lorinda Cauley
Singing Bee! A Collection of Favorite Children's Songs
Tail Feathers from Mother Goose: The Opie Rhyme Book, Iona and Peter Opie
Tomie De Paola's Mother Goose, Tomie De Paola
A Week of Lullabies, Helen Plotz
Wendy Watson's Mother Goose, Wendy Watson

Hittin' the Road

Despite what your mother or mother-in-law might tell you, you can take your
baby out at any age. The trick is in knowing how to dress him.

One of the great myths about babies is that you have to bundle them up
like Nanook of the North every time you take them out of the house. Here's the
truth: overdressed babies are at risk of getting heat stroke, which can result in
abnormally high fevers and even convulsions. This risk is especially high if
you're taking the baby out in a sling, backpack, or frontpack, where he'll be
even hotter.

Of course, underdressing can be a problem, too. The answer is to dress your
baby just as you would dress yourself (except that you're probably not going
to wear any of those cute little booties). When the weather's cold, it helps to
dress the baby in various layers rather than one or two very heavy items. That
way you can remove a layer or two if the baby gets overheated.

Most important, because you're the grown-up, you're going to have to pay
close attention. If you underdress your baby, he'll probably let you know about
it; babies usually complain loudly when they're too cold. Babies who are too
hot, though, tend *not* to complain, preferring, instead, to lie there listlessly.

SUMMER

For the first six months, your baby should be kept far away from direct sun-
light. Because babies' skin is at its thinnest and lightest during this period,
even a little sun can do a lot of damage. This applies to babies of all races
and skin tones.

When you go out, dress your baby in lightweight and light-colored long-sleeved shirts and long pants. From the time they were a few months old, neither of my kids would let me put any kind of hat anywhere near them. But if you can get your baby to wear a cute hat with a wide brim, so much the better. And if you're brave enough to try putting sunglasses on her, get the kind that shield her eyes from UVA and UVB rays. For extra protection, consider getting a parasol or sunshade for your stroller and try to stay indoors during the hottest parts of the day (about 11 A.M. to 3 P.M.).

When you're putting together your supplies for an outdoor summertime excursion, throw in a sweater and some warm pants for the baby. Sounds a little strange, but if you step into any kind of air-conditioned building (such as a supermarket or your office building) after having been outside for a while, you're going to feel awfully cold—and so will the baby.

Oh, and by the way, if you were thinking that your baby can't get a sunburn on a cloudy or overcast day, think again. Studies have shown that 60 percent of the sun's UV rays make their way down here, regardless of clouds, fog, or anything else.

Skin Problems

SUN

Despite all your precautions and good intentions, your baby may still end up with a minor sun-related condition:

♦ **Sunburn.** If it's minor, cover the affected area with a cool compress. If there are blisters, if the baby is running a fever, or if he's listless or nonresponsive, call your doctor immediately.

♦ **Prickly heat (heat rash).** A direct result of overdressing, prickly heat looks like tiny red blisters on a flushed area. It occurs anywhere sweat can build up: where the neck meets the shoulders, under the arms, inside elbows and knees, inside diapers. If your baby has heat rash, try to keep him as cool as possible. Lotions and creams probably won't help much, but putting a cool, damp washcloth or some cornstarch on the affected area may make your baby more comfortable.

INSECTS

The sun isn't the only potentially dangerous element that comes out in the summer. Here are some tips for preventing your baby from being consumed by insects:

♦ Don't use any kind of scented powders, lotions, or even diaper wipes. Bugs love them.

Sunscreen

Until she's six months old, don't use any sunscreen on your baby at all (that's why it's so important to keep infants out of the sun). Because they are usually so filled with chemicals, sunscreens frequently cause allergic reactions.

After six months, the risk of an allergic reaction from sunscreen is much lower, but stick with one that's unscented, alcohol- and PABA-free, and hypoallergenic, or made specially for infants. Hawaiian Tropic, Johnson & Johnson, and Water Babies all make acceptable formulas.

Lube your baby up with sunscreen about half an hour before going outside, and add some more every three hours or so. Pay special attention to feet, hands, legs, and arms—even if they're completely covered. Socks can roll down, and sleeves and pant legs can hike up all by themselves, exposing baby's skin to the elements.

♦ Avoid insect repellent if at all possible. A long-sleeved shirt and long pants can provide just about the same level of protection and are a lot easier on infant skin.
♦ Stay away from clothes with floral patterns: most bugs aren't smart enough to tell the difference between a real flower and your equally delicious flower-covered child. Light colors are far less attractive to bugs than dark colors.

DIAPER RASH

In the pre-disposable-diaper era, when a baby urinated the moisture stayed right there against her skin. Partly because of the acid in urine and partly because it's uncomfortable to sit in something wet, the baby would soon start complaining. And if she made what my older daughter used to call "a big dirty" (a bowel movement), her discomfort was greater, and her complaints voiced sooner. This raised the chances that she'd get changed fairly quickly.

But with disposables, a lot of the moisture is whisked away from the baby (just like in the commercials) and converted into some kind of nonliquid gel. Still, the digestive acids in the baby's waste, especially in her stool, continue to irritate her skin until—voilà!—diaper rash. But because the baby isn't uncomfortable enough to complain, her diapers somehow don't manage to get changed quite as often.

Unlike sunburn or insect bites, no matter what you do or how hard you try, one of these days your baby is going to get diaper rash. Just about the only thing you can do to keep it to a minimum is to check your baby's diapers every few hours and change them even if they're only slightly wet. Also:

♦ If you're using cloth diapers, don't use rubber or plastic pants. Your baby's bottom needs good air circulation.

♦ When diaper rash develops, let your baby frolic for a few minutes sans diaper (on a towel, perhaps, just in case . . .). The extra air circulation will help.

♦ Apply some diaper cream with each change, but be especially gentle: irritated skin doesn't like to be rubbed. A piece of advice: after you've applied diaper rash cream to the baby's bottom, wipe any residual cream on your fingers onto the inside of the diaper. If any of the cream gets onto the plastic fasteners of a disposable diaper, they won't stick to the diaper.

Notes:

MONTHS

Born to Be...

What's Going On with the Baby

Physically

♦ Lying on her back, she can now track moving objects, coordinating the activities of her eyes and head as well as an adult can.

♦ She's making better use of her hands, using them to finger each other, and to grasp small objects (most of which immediately end up in her mouth). But she hasn't yet figured out what to do with her opposable thumb. So, for the next few months at least, she won't be using it much, making her grasping a little clumsy.

♦ By the end of this month, though, she will have figured out that the two sides of her body are separate—a discovery she's glad to demonstrate by passing things back and forth between her hands.

♦ While on her tummy, she can lift her head 90 degrees and prop herself up on her forearms.

♦ She may be able to roll from her tummy to her side, and may occasionally make it onto her back.

♦ She still tries to stand when you pull her up, and when she's sitting, her back is straight and her head hardly wobbles.

Intellectually

♦ Your baby is developing a physical sense of her body, recognizing that her hands and feet are extensions of herself. And she'll spend a great deal of time every day using her hands to explore her face, her mouth, and whatever other parts of her body she can reach.

◆ She can retain objects in her hands voluntarily.

◆ She's beginning the long process of understanding cause and effect relationships. If she accidentally kicks a toy and it squeaks, she may try to kick it again, hoping to get the same reaction.

◆ She's begun to draw small distinctions between similar objects. She can clearly tell the difference between a real face and a picture of one, and she can distinguish nearby objects from distant ones.

◆ She is also starting to differentiate herself from some other objects in her world. She may, for example, find a special toy particularly soothing.

Verbally

◆ The amount of time your baby spends crying has decreased dramatically and she's just about ready to hold up her end of a conversation.

◆ When she hears a sound—especially a voice—she actively searches for it with her eyes.

◆ And if you wait a few seconds after saying something to her, she may "answer" you, making ample use of her expanding vocabulary of squeals, chuckles, chortles, giggles, and clicks.

◆ She's trying as hard as she can to imitate one or two sounds and, if she's got something on her mind, may take the initiative and start a "conversation" with you.

Emotionally/Socially

◆ Overall, your baby is a pretty happy kid, smiling regularly and spontaneously and anticipating pleasurable encounters by vigorously kicking her arms and legs.

◆ She's also so anxious to socialize that she can actually suppress other interests in order to play. If you talk to her while she's eating, for example, she'll gladly stop for half an hour or so to chat.

◆ She now tries to extend her playtime by laughing or holding her gaze on a desired object, and she may protest loudly if you stop doing what she wants you to.

◆ Despite this hedonistic streak, she's still got clear preferences among playmates. Some will be able to soothe her, others won't.

◆ This is an extremely busy developmental time for your baby, and you may notice some interruption in her sleep patterns as she wakes up in the middle of the night to practice her new tricks.

What You're Going Through

Reevaluating Your Relationship with Your Job

Remember the shift in focus and priorities we talked about last month—from self to family? Well, once that shift has begun, the very next thing most new fathers do is take a long, hard look at their jobs.

In a small number of cases, fathers make a renewed commitment to their jobs—longer hours, increased productivity, more responsibility—motivated by a need to provide for their growing families. A far more common scenario, however, is the one Bruce Drobeck found in his research. Most new fathers, he says, "were looking for ways to reduce or restructure their work hours in order to achieve a balance between work and family."

This, of course, flies in the face of a lot of the stereotypes we often hear about fathers. But if you don't believe me, consider the results of a few national polls:

♦ 65 percent of fathers in one national poll said they believe they are being asked to sacrifice too much family time for the workplace.

♦ 57 percent of the men surveyed at one major corporation (up from 37 percent five years earlier) wanted work-schedule flexibility that would allow them to spend more time with their families.

♦ A recent survey by *Forbes* magazine found that 30 percent of fathers with kids under twelve had personally turned down a job promotion or transfer because it would have reduced the time they spend with their families.

Based on these statistics, it shouldn't come as much of a surprise that, as researcher John Snarey found, "a majority of husbands now experience fathering as more psychologically rewarding . . . than their occupations."

However, lest you think that all this is just a bunch of optimistic rhetoric, here's an example of the lengths to which some new fathers will go in order to spend more time with their families. A recent study by the Families and Work Institute stated that "some men had told friends at work they were going to a bar when in fact they were going home to care for their children."

Coming to Terms with Breastfeeding

Before their babies are born, nearly all expectant fathers feel that breastfeeding is the best way to feed a baby and that their partners should do so as long as possible. After the baby comes, new fathers still feel that breast is best, but many are also feeling a little ambivalent.

Most new fathers feel that breastfeeding "perpetuates the exclusive relationship the mother and infant experienced during pregnancy," writes Dr. Pamela Jordan, one of the few researchers ever to explore the effects of breastfeeding on men.

Given all this, says Dr. Jordan, a new father is likely to experience:

♦ A diminished opportunity to develop a relationship with his child.

♦ A sense of inadequacy.

♦ A feeling that the baby has come between him and his partner.

♦ A feeling that nothing he does to satisfy his child can ever compete with his partner's breasts.

♦ A sense of relief when his partner weans the baby, giving him the opportunity to "catch up."

♦ A belief in what Jordan calls the "hormonal advantage theory"—the idea that women are born with certain knowledge and skills that give them an advantage in parenting, including guaranteed success with breastfeeding.

SIPRESS

Whether or not you're experiencing these or any other less-than-completely-positive feelings, there's a good chance that your partner is having a few ambivalent feelings of her own about breastfeeding. Here are some of the things she may be feeling:

+ Exhaustion. It may look easy and relaxing to you, but nursing a baby is tough work.
+ Despite the images of smiling, happy nursing mothers, your partner simply may not be enjoying the experience. And if she isn't, she may be feeling guilty or inadequate. (Just goes to show you that fathers aren't the only ones boxed in by socialization.)
+ She may resent the way nursing interferes with some of the other things she'd like to do.
+ She may want to run as far away from the baby as possible. If so, she's also likely to feel guilty or selfish (socialization again . . . mothers are always supposed to be happy to be with their children).
+ She may not be interested in answering your questions about the process. (I had a million for my wife: How does it feel? How much comes out in each feeding? Does the milk come out from one hole or more than one?)

"Preparing a meal and feeding someone is a powerful symbolic act," writes

Dr. Jordan. "Feeding the infant is often perceived by parents as the most important aspect of infant care, the most meaningful interaction." If your partner is breastfeeding, there's no question that you're at a bit of a disadvantage when it comes to feeding the baby. There are, however, a few ways you can help your partner and yourself make breastfeeding as pleasant an experience as possible for everyone:

♦ You can bottle-feed your baby with breast milk if your partner is willing to express some. But don't insist on this. Many women find expressing milk— manually or with a pump—uncomfortable or even painful.

♦ Don't take it personally if your baby doesn't seem interested in taking a bottle from you. Some babies need a few days to get used to the idea of sucking on a plastic nipple instead of a real one. Other babies, like my younger daughter, simply refuse to take a bottle at all. But don't give up without a fight. Plastic nipples—like real ones—come in all sorts of shapes and sizes. So you may have to do a little experimenting before you and your baby discover the kind she likes best (which may or may not have anything in common with the kind you like best).

♦ Make sure you get some private time with your baby for activities that provide regular skin-to-skin contact, such as bathing, cuddling, playing, putting to bed, and even changing diapers. According to Dr. Jordan, establishing rituals like these with your baby may help you feel that "the mother does not have exclusive rights to a special relationship." It can also help your partner by giving her some needed time off.

♦ Compare notes with other men whose partners breastfed their babies.

For Women Only (you can read this, but only if you promise to show it to your partner when you're done)
"The breastfeeding mother has the control of parenting and must realize that she has the power to invite the father in or exclude him," writes Dr. Pamela Jordan. "She can play a vital role in establishing exclusive father-infant time, often while simultaneously meeting her own needs for time away and alone. Just as the father is viewed as the primary support of the mother-infant relationship, the mother is the primary support of the father-infant relationship . . . supporting the father during breastfeeding may help improve his, and consequently, the mother's, satisfaction with breastfeeding, the duration of breastfeeding, and the adaptation of both parents to parenthood."

Worried That Your Life Will Never Be the Same Again (It Won't)

Before my kids were born, just about everybody my wife and I knew with kids pulled us aside and tried to warn us that our lives would change forever once we became parents. They told us about how hard it is to shift from worrying about only ourselves to being responsible for the safety and well-being of a completely helpless little person. They told us that we'd lose a lot of sleep and even more privacy. And they told us that we'd better go to a lot of movies and read a stack of books because we might not have another chance for a while. Everything everyone said was absolutely correct, but none of it really prepared us for our transition to parenthood.

What I often find most interesting about the changes I underwent when I became a father is the way my memories of my prefatherhood past have been subtly altered. It's not that I can't or don't remember life before children, it's just that that life, in retrospect, seems somehow incomplete.

I have clear, fond memories of taking long walks on the beach by myself, sleeping in all day, and going out at midnight for a beer with friends—things I haven't done much since becoming a father. It's as though those things happened to someone else, however. I don't really miss my other life, but in a way I wish I could have shared it with my children (not the beers, perhaps, but the walks on the beach and the sleeping in).

You and Your Baby

Your Baby's Temperament

About forty years ago a husband-and-wife team of psychiatrists, Stella Chess and Alexander Thomas, theorized that children are born with a set of nine fundamental behavioral and emotional traits they called "temperamental qualities." These qualities, which experts now believe remain fairly consistent throughout life, combine differently for each child and determine, to a great extent, a child's personality and whether he will be "easy" or "challenging." In addition, Chess and Thomas found that a child's temperament has a major influence on his parents' behavior and attitudes.

Over the past few decades, Chess and Thomas's original research in temperament has been expanded, refined, and improved upon. Here, then, are the nine temperament traits, adapted from Chess and Thomas, the Temperament Program at the Center for Parenting Excellence, and the work of Jim Cameron, head of The Preventive Ounce, a nonprofit mental health organization for children.

The Nine Temperament Traits of Babies

APPROACHING
- separate easily from parents
- are excited to meet and interact with new people
- greet new foods eagerly
- seem perfectly "at home" in new situations

WITHDRAWING
- are usually shy, cling to their parents in new situations or around strangers
- have difficulty separating from parents
- need time to warm up to new experiences
- may be extremely picky eaters and spit out food with new taste sensations

FAST ADAPTING
- fall asleep easily and without fussing, no matter where they are
- don't mind changes in routines
- can be fed easily by different people
- don't mind being handled by different people or passed around
- smile back quickly when talked to

SLOW ADAPTING
- may refuse to fall asleep in a strange place (or even a moderately familiar one like grandma and grandpa's)
- are slow to get back to sleep after being awakened
- don't like being picked up and held by strangers
- take a long time to warm up to new situations, and once upset, may take a long time to calm down

LOW INTENSITY
- display their emotions, but are often hard to read
- have subdued moods
- seem fairly nonchalant

HIGH INTENSITY
- react strongly (positively or negatively) to strangers, loud noises, bright lights
- do everything—shrieking with delight or crying—so loudly it hurts your ears

POSITIVE MOOD
- laugh and smile at just about everything
- are happy even when having their diapers changed
- seem genuinely happy to see you

NEGATIVE MOOD
- cry when being changed
- are fussy or cranky most of the time
- whimper or cry a lot, sometimes seemingly for no reason
- complain during hair brushing

LOW ACTIVITY
- seem content to lie still while nursing or getting changed
- will sit calmly in the car seat
- prefer less physical play (swings instead of wrestling)

HIGH ACTIVITY
- move around a lot while sleeping, frequently kicking their blankets off
- move around a lot while awake, and are hard to dress, change, bathe, or feed
- often reach physical developmental milestones earlier than lower-activity kids

PREDICTABLE	UNPREDICTABLE
♦ get hungry, tired, and move their bowels at about the same times every day	♦ may or may not take naps
	♦ have frequent sleep problems and get up several times during the night
♦ love regular eating and bedtime schedules	♦ may not be hungry at mealtimes and may want to eat at different times every day
♦ struggle with changes in eating and sleep routines	♦ have irregular bowel movements

HIGH SENSORY THRESHOLD (OBLIVIOUS)	LOW SENSORY THRESHOLD (VERY AWARE)
♦ love loud events (basketball games, circuses, bands . . .)	♦ are easily overstimulated
♦ aren't bothered by wet or dirty diapers	♦ are awakened easily by gentle touch or by turning on lights
♦ are emotionally stable	♦ may get extremely upset at loud noises
♦ don't seem to be able to differentiate between two voices	♦ notice tiny variations in the taste of food
♦ aren't bothered by clothing labels or scratchy fabrics	♦ are extremely uncomfortable in wet or dirty diapers
♦ don't seem bothered by pain	♦ are very sensitive to fabrics, labels, and the fit of their clothes

LOW DISTRACTIBILITY	HIGH DISTRACTIBILITY
♦ are quite hard to soothe	♦ have short attention spans
♦ seem completely oblivious to interruptions (noise, familiar voices) when involved in something important (like nursing)	♦ are easily distracted while nursing
	♦ are easily soothed when upset

HIGH PERSISTENCE	LOW PERSISTENCE
♦ are able to amuse themselves for a few minutes at a time	♦ can't amuse themselves for very long in crib or playpen
♦ like to practice new motor skills (like rolling from back to front) for a minute or more	♦ have short attention spans and are frustrated easily, even by simple tasks
♦ pay close attention (for more than a minute) to rattles and mobiles	♦ quickly lose interest in playing, even with favorite toys
♦ pay close attention to other children when playing	♦ won't spend much time working on new skills (rolling over, sitting up)
♦ cry when you stop playing with them	

1. Approach/Withdrawal: Your child's usual *initial* reaction to a new experience, such as meeting a new person, tasting a new food, or being in a new situation.
2. Adaptability: Similar to Approach/Withdrawal, but deals with your child's longer-term reactions to changes in routines or expectations, new places, and new ideas.
3. Intensity: The amount of energy a child commonly uses to express emotions—both positive and negative.
4. Mood: Your child's general mood—happy or fussy—over the course of a typical day.
5. Activity level: The amount of energy your child puts into everything he does.
6. Regularity: The day-to-day predictability of your baby's hunger, sleeping, and filling diapers.
7. Sensitivity: Your baby's sensitivity to pain, noise, temperature change, lights, odors, flavors, textures, and emotions. Note: it's quite possible for your baby to be highly sensitive to one sensation (bright lights, for example) but not at all sensitive to others (noise).
8. Distractibility: How easy is it to change the focus of your baby's attention.
9. Persistence: Similar to Distractibility, but goes beyond the initial reaction and concerns the length of time your baby will spend trying to overcome obstacles or distractions.

Now that you know what to look for, spend a few minutes rating your baby on the following scale. And have your partner do it, too.

TRAIT	RATING						
Approach/Withdrawal	Approaching	1	2	3	4	5	Withdrawing
Adaptability	Fast	1	2	3	4	5	Slow
Intensity	Low	1	2	3	4	5	High
Mood	Positive	1	2	3	4	5	Negative
Activity Level	Low	1	2	3	4	5	High
Regularity	Predictable	1	2	3	4	5	Unpredictable
Sensitivity	Oblivious	1	2	3	4	5	Very Aware
Distractibility	Low	1	2	3	4	5	High
Persistence	High	1	2	3	4	5	Low

ENFANT TERRIBLE.

MUELLER

If you have a lot of 1s and 2s, you're one lucky guy. You've got an "easy" child (about 40 percent of parents do), and having an easy child is, well, easy. The baby's always smiling and happy, sleeps through the night, eats at the same time every day, and loves playing and meeting new people. When he does get upset or fussy, you can usually calm him down almost immediately. You're madly in love with your baby and you're feeling confident about your parenting skills.

But if you ended up with a lot of 4s and 5s, you most likely have a "challenging" child (only about 10 percent of parents do), and things are not nearly as rosy. She doesn't sleep through the night, has trouble eating, freaks out at the slightest noise or change in her surroundings, cries for hours at a time (and nothing you try seems to make it any better), and is generally fussy. Meanwhile, you're exhausted and depressed, angry at the baby for her "malicious" behavior, embarrassed at the way people stare at your unhappy child, guilty about your unparental feelings, and jealous of your friends and their easy babies. In short, you're not finding your parenting experience very satisfying, you're discouraged and frustrated, and you think you must be a complete failure as a father. You may even feel trapped and fantasize about running away.

As bad as it sounds, there are some things you can do to help you overcome a lot of your frustration and negative feelings:

♦ Recognize that challenging children are challenging because of their innate makeup. Their temperament exists at birth. It's not their fault, it's not your fault, and it's not your partner's fault. It's just the way things are.

♦ Stop blaming yourself, your partner, or your baby. There's probably nothing wrong with any of you. The problem is that the way you're interacting with your child simply isn't working.

♦ Get to know your child's—and your own—temperament and look for similarities and differences. If you're both Highly Distractible, you may never get through that book you're reading—and neither of you will care. But if you're Highly Approaching and the baby is Highly Withdrawing, you may have some real problems taking her to meet your boss for the first time.

At the very least, these steps will enable you to modify your approaches to your child's behavior and to anticipate and avoid conflicts before they occur. The result will be a far happier, more loving, and more satisfying relationship with your child. Guaranteed.

Putting Your Knowledge of Temperament to Good Use

Following are some of the most common, difficult-to-handle traits you're likely to encounter during your baby's first year, along with some suggestions for how to handle them, loosely based on the work of researchers Stanley Turecki and Leslie Tonner.

INITIAL WITHDRAWAL/SLOW ADAPTABILITY

Just because your baby initially spits out new foods and refuses to play with new toys doesn't mean he'll never change. Before you give up, try gently introducing new foods a few times at different meals, and give the baby a chance to "meet" a new toy from a distance before letting him touch it. (This process will help you figure out whether your child is Withdrawing and Slow-Adapting or has a Low Sensory Threshold.)

Your Withdrawing/Slow-Adapting baby will probably begin experiencing *stranger anxiety* (see pages 149–50) earlier—and it will last longer—than more Approaching and Fast-Adapting babies. Tell new visitors, and even those the baby knows a little bit, not to approach too quickly, not to try to pick him up right away, and not to take it personally if the baby reacts negatively.

One warning: Think about your baby's temperament before making any major changes in your appearance. Shaving your beard, getting a haircut, or even re-placing your glasses with contact lenses can trigger a strong, negative reaction. When my older daughter was six months old, her baby-sitter—whom she absolutely adored—got a haircut, and it took her more than a week to recover.

HIGH INTENSITY

Short of leaving the room or getting ear plugs (both of which are perfectly reasonable approaches), there's not much you can do about your High-Intensity baby.

NEGATIVE MOOD

Not much can make you happier than going out with a smiling, happy baby. But a baby who isn't a smiler, and who whimpers and cries all the time, can be a real challenge to your self-confidence. It's hard to take pleasure in a baby with a Negative Mood, or even to feel proud of her. And it's certainly tempting to think that if the baby doesn't smile at you all the time, she doesn't love you.

If you're feeling this way, resist the urge to get angry with your baby for her whining, or to "get even" with her by withholding your love. (I know it sounds silly, but it happens.) The truth is that the lack of a smile doesn't necessarily mean there's a lack of love. And the whining *will* subside as your baby's verbal skills improve, enabling her to get your attention in more productive ways.

HIGH ACTIVITY

Because your High-Activity baby will spend his sleeping moments doing laps in his crib, it's important to install some big, soft bumpers (pads designed to protect babies' heads from banging into the bars). You'll also need to make sure there's nothing in the crib (or nearby) that could fall on top of the baby's head. And, if your house tends to be a little cold at night, dress the baby in something thick so he'll be warm when he kicks the covers off.

Never, never leave your baby unattended—even for a second—on a changing table or bed; she could very well roll off. Once, when my older daughter was seven months old, I was tickling her in her bassinet when the phone (located about three feet away) rang. I stepped over, said "Hello," and heard a loud thump behind me: my daughter, who had never given any indication that she could pull herself up, had done exactly that, and toppled over the side of the bassinet. No harm was done, but we never used that bassinet again.

UNPREDICTABILITY

Since your Unpredictable baby seems to be eating, sleeping, and filling his diaper at random, it's up to you to try to establish a regular schedule. Although he may not want to eat, try to feed him something at times that are more convenient for you. If you schedule meals at the same times every day, you may be able to help him create a modified routine.

When it comes to getting your baby to sleep, establishing a routine is also important. When you go into his room at night, don't turn on the lights, don't pick him up, don't play, and get out as soon as you can. Once you stumble on a getting-back-to-sleep routine, stick with it. If your baby's sleep irregularities are truly serious, you and your partner should divide up the night, each taking a shift while the other sleeps. If that doesn't help, talk with your pediatrician about a mild sedative. For the baby, not you.

LOW SENSORY THRESHOLD

For the first few months of a Low-Sensory-Threshold baby's life, you'll never know what's going to set her off. Sounds, smells, and sensations you might hardly notice can cause her to explode into tears: turning on the car radio, the crowd applauding at a basketball game (yes, you can take babies to basketball games), even too many toys in her crib.

One way to make your baby's life a little less jarring is to modify the amount and type of stimulation in her environment. Avoid neon colors when decorating her room, get opaque drapes to keep daytime light out during nap time, and don't play actively with her right before bedtime. When dressing your baby, stay away from tight clothes, brand-new clothes (they're often too stiff), wool, synthetic fabrics, or anything with a rough texture. Cotton blends usually offer the best combination of washability and softness. And be sure to clip off scratchy labels and tags.

HIGH DISTRACTIBILITY AND LOW PERSISTENCE

These traits are usually not much of a problem for you or your baby at this stage.

For most readers, this discussion of temperament should be sufficient to identify and begin to deal with their child's behavior patterns. But if you're seriously concerned about your child's temperament, or would be interested in exploring the subject in greater detail, I suggest you contact Temperament Talk, in Portland, Oregon, or Jim Cameron at The Preventive Ounce.

Family Matters

Sleeping Tight

We all love our children, but let's face it, sometimes we want them to go to sleep—and stay that way for a while. There are all sorts of factors (many of which are beyond your control) that influence whether your child will be a "good" sleeper or a "bad" one. Fortunately, though, there are a few rules of thumb that can help tilt the odds in your favor:

"And so the big bad wolf ate Little Red Riding Hood, Hansel and Gretel, Cinderella, and the three little pigs, and that was the end of fairy tales forever. Now good night!"

♦ Don't become the baby's sleep transition object. Baby's last waking memory should be of her crib or something familiar in it (blankie, toy, a picture on the wall). That way, if she wakes up in the middle of the night, she'll see the familiar object and be able to associate it with sleep. If you were the last thing she saw before dropping off, she'll want you again, even if you happen to be sleeping.

♦ It's perfectly natural for babies to fuss or be restless for fifteen or twenty minutes after being put down. (Please remember that fussing is one thing, screaming is another. If the baby begins to really wail, pick her up and soothe her, but try to get her back in her crib while she's still awake. It's absolutely impossible to spoil a baby by picking her up or soothing her in the first three or four months of life.)

♦ Keep nighttime activity to a minimum. Whether your baby is sleeping with you or not, she needs to learn that nighttime is for sleeping, not for playing.

♦ Don't turn on the lights. If the baby wakes up for a middle-of-the-night breast or bottle, do it in the dark.

♦ Don't change diapers unless you absolutely have to (such as when you're trying to treat a particularly nasty case of diaper rash). In most cases, your baby will be perfectly fine until the morning.

♦ Establish a routine. You'll need to make up your own, depending on what works best for you. Here's a fairly simple routine that is good for babies this age as well as for toddlers: change diapers, get sleepsuit on, read a story or two, go around the room and say "goodnight" to all the toys and animals, give a kiss goodnight, and into bed.

◆ When your baby is about six months old, start leaving the door to her room open. Kids this age get scared if they feel they're trapped in a small space, especially if they aren't sure you're just outside the door.

◆ In case of nightmares or other middle-of-the-night scares, respond promptly and be as reassuring as possible. Unless your child is hysterical with fear, try to keep things brief and resist the urge to take the baby out of the crib. You can do a lot of soothing by rubbing the baby's back or head—all from your side of the bars.

◆ During the day, gently wake up—and entertain—your baby if she tries to nap more than two or three hours at a stretch. The idea is to make her longest sleep of the day occur at night.

But What about Those Middle-of-the-Night Wake-Ups?

The most common reason babies wake up in the middle of the night is that they want to eat. If your partner is breastfeeding, do everything you can to stay in bed and let her handle things. I realize that this sounds positively insensitive, but the truth is that there's really nothing you can do to help out. If your partner wants some adult company (and who wouldn't?), try not to give in. Instead, offer to give her a few extra hours of sleep while you handle the early-morning child-care shift (which usually lasts a lot longer than a 2 A.M. feeding).

Of course, if you're bottle-feeding your baby (either with formula or expressed breast milk), you should do your fair share of the feedings. And since there's no sense in both you and your partner getting up at the same time, you

---

Naps and Sleep Schedules

At four months your baby has probably only recently settled into a regular sleep routine. Every baby has her own sleeping schedule, but a typical one for a baby this age might include a ten-hour stretch at night plus, if you're lucky, two two-hour naps—one midmorning, the other midafternoon.

Keep an eye on these naps, however; if they get too late, they may start upsetting the night-sleeping routine. You can't expect a baby to take a nap from 4 to 6 P.M. and then go to bed for the night at 7.

should be able to negotiate breakfast in bed (or at least a couple of hours of sleep) on those days when you do the 2 A.M. feeding.

Sometimes, no matter what you do, your baby is going to wake up at two or three in the morning for no other reason than to stay awake for a few hours and check things out. As with the feeding situations, try to split the entertainment duty as much as you can (unless one of you really needs to catch up on TV reruns or order a slicing, dicing, memory-improving, income-boosting workout machine).

No matter what it is that gets your baby (and you) up at three thirty in the morning, be sure to keep your middle-of-the-night encounters as boring as possible. Until they're old enough to have sex, kids need to know that nighttime is for sleeping.

Sleeping Arrangements

As hard as it may be to imagine, there exists a rather basic parenting issue that regularly generates even more controversy than the disposable versus cloth diapers debate: whether or not to have your child sleep in the same bed as you and your partner.

The argument goes something like this: Proponents of the "family bed" say that kids are being forced to be independent too early, that human evolution simply can't keep pace with the new demands our culture is placing on its children. "Proximity to parental sounds, smells, heat, and movement during the night is precisely what the human infant's immature system expects and needs," says James McKenna, an anthropologist and sleep researcher. They also add that in most countries (comprising about 80 percent of the world's population), parents and children sleep in the same bed.

Opponents of the family bed, however, say that what works in other countries doesn't always work here. In America early independence is critical, and babies should therefore quickly learn to be away from their parents, especially if both work and the children have to be in day care.

Fortunately (or unfortunately, depending on where you stand on the issue), there's absolutely no consensus on which of these two opposing views is the "right" one. And just to make sure that there's no real way to decide this issue once and for all, there's no serious scientific data supporting either position.

Our older daughter slept in a bassinet in our room for a month or so until we moved her into her own room. Our younger daughter, however, slept in bed with us for six months before being asked to leave. Personally, I kind of liked being able to snuggle up with a warm, smooth baby, but after being kicked in the head, stomach, back, face, and chest every night for six months I was glad to go back to an adults-only sleeping arrangement.

Here are some of the most common issues that come up in discussions of the family bed:

+ **Independence.** Critics of family sleeping claim that parents who let their kids sleep with them are spoiling their children, who will grow up clingy and dependent. "Sleeping alone is an important part of a child's learning to be able to separate from his parents without anxiety and to see himself as an independent individual," writes Dr. Richard Ferber, one of the most well-respected anti-family-bed people around. Proponents of family sleeping, however, make nearly the opposite claim, maintaining that before a child can become independent she must feel that the world is a safe place and that her needs will be met. Kids who sleep in a family bed, proponents argue, turn out to be more independent, more confident, and more self-assured than those who don't.

+ **Sleep: the baby's.** Despite what you might think, co-sleeping children tend to sleep more lightly than children who sleep alone (blankets rustling and parents turning over in bed wake them up). But light sleeping isn't necessarily a bad thing. In fact, there seems to be a correlation between lighter sleep and a lower incidence of SIDS.

+ **Sleep: yours.** It's perfectly normal for even the soundest-sleeping kids to wake up every three or four hours for a quick look around the room. The vast majority (about 70 percent) soothe themselves back to sleep after a minute or two. But about 30 percent will spot something they just have to play with (you or your partner, for example), and they're up for hours.

+ **Safety.** Many parents are afraid that they'll accidentally roll over their sleeping child if the whole family is sharing the same bed. While this is a perfectly legitimate concern, most adults—even while asleep—have a highly developed sense of where they are. It's probably been quite a while since you fell out of bed in the middle of the night. However, a recent study published in the *New England Journal of Medicine* found that adult overlying (non-alcohol and non-drug-related) was the probable cause of death in almost 20 percent of infants whose death had initially been attributed to SIDS.

+ **Sexual spontaneity.** No kidding. But there are plenty of other places to make love besides your bed.

+ **Breastfeeding.** There's no question that it's a lot easier for a nursing mother to reach across her bed for the baby than to get up and stagger down the hall. Problems arise, however, when fathers feel (and they often

do) displaced by the nursing baby and decide that the only place to get
a good night's sleep is on the couch.

♦ **Think before you start.** Once your baby has been sleeping in your bed
for six to eight months, it's going to be awfully hard to get her out if you
change your mind.

A Few Things to Consider If You're Thinking about Sharing Your Bed with Your Child

♦ Keep politics out of your decision-making. Sleep with your child because
you and your partner want to, not because you feel you have to.

♦ Don't be embarrassed. You're not being soft, negligent, or overindulgent—
it's a choice made by millions of fine parents.

♦ Make sure your bed is large enough to accommodate everyone. (But no
waterbeds—baby could roll between you and the mattress.) Put the bed
against the wall and have the baby sleep on the wall side, or get a guard
rail if she's going to sleep on the outside edge. And remember, overly
soft mattresses and pillows may pose a risk of suffocation.

♦ Make sure everyone's toenails are trimmed.

♦ Rethink your decision right now if you're obese, you drink or take any
medication that might make you hard to wake up, or if you're generally
such a sound sleeper that you're worried you might roll on top of your
baby without noticing.

A Few Things to Consider If You're Thinking about Not Sharing Your Bed with Your Child

♦ Don't feel guilty. You're not a bad or selfish parent for not doing it.

♦ There is absolutely no evidence that sleeping with your child will speed up
the bonding/attachment process.

♦ It's okay to make an occasional exception, such as when a child is ill or has
had a frightening experience.

♦ If you're making your decision because of safety issues, you may be able to
compromise by setting up the baby's crib in your bedroom.

Work and Family

What's Going On with the Baby

Physically

♦ This month's big discovery is, yes, toes. And just as your baby spent hours fondling and sucking his own fingers, he'll repeat the process with his lower extremities.

♦ He's getting a lot stronger and is now able to roll from his stomach to his back at will. He can also get himself from his tummy to his hands and knees. Once there, he may rock back and forth as if anxious for some kind of race to begin.

♦ When you pull him to a standing position, he'll try to help you out by leaning his head forward and bending at the waist. Once standing, he may stamp his feet up and down.

♦ He's almost able to sit without support and can now pick up objects while sitting.

♦ His hands continue to get more coordinated. He now plays with a toy in either hand and can turn his wrist (it's harder than it sounds), thus enabling him to get a better look at what he's picked up.

♦ There are now longer and more regular intervals between feedings and bowel movements.

Intellectually

♦ For the past four months, your baby's world has been "a series of things that mysteriously disappear and reappear," writes child development expert Frank Caplan. But now he's no longer content to sit back and stare at objects, nor is he satisfied when you put something in his hand. In an attempt to actively engage in his world, he's starting to reach for things. Watch carefully as he looks back and forth between an object and his hand—inching the hand slowly toward the object. As mundane as it sounds, reaching is a critical intellectual stage, introducing the baby to the idea that, says Caplan, "things are beyond and apart and, therefore, separate" from him.

♦ Handling and turning an object teaches the baby that even though something looks different from different angles, its shape remains the same.

♦ With these newfound skills, the baby will now anticipate (and get excited by) seeing only a small part of a familiar object and will try to move small obstacles out of his way. He's also learning that objects can move, and he may lean over to find a toy he's dropped instead of staring at his hand. But if the object is out of his sight for more than just a few seconds, it ceases to exist and he forgets about it.

Verbally

♦ It's finally happened: your baby is babbling. Besides the vowel sounds (*eee, aaa, ayy*) he's been making, he's added a few consonants (*bbb, ddd, mmm*) to the mix.

♦ He's found his voice's volume switch and will practice modulating his voice.

♦ Although he's still trying to imitate more of the voice sounds you make to him, the noises he produces sound nothing like actual language.

♦ He's so delighted with his newfound language skills that he'll babble for 20 to 30 minutes at a stretch. Don't worry if you're not there to enjoy it— he's perfectly content to talk to his toys or, in a pinch, to himself.

♦ He may understand, and respond to, his name.

Emotionally/Socially

♦ He's capable of expressing a growing number of emotions: fear, anger, disgust, and satisfaction. He'll cry if you put him down and calm down if you pick him up.

♦ He also has—and readily expresses—strong preferences for toys and people. And he deliberately imitates faces and gestures.

♦ If he feels you're not paying enough attention to him, he'll try to interrupt whatever you're doing with a yelp or a cry. If he does start crying, you can usually stop his tears just by talking to him.

- ♦ He knows the difference between familiar people and strangers, and associates friends with his pleasure.
- ♦ Unfortunately, he doesn't remember that his friends started off (to him, at least) as strangers. Consequently, he's a little slow to warm to new people.
- ♦ He may spend some time trying to soothe himself—either by talking to himself or by clutching a favorite toy.

What You're Going Through

Worried about Doing Things Wrong

Just a few months ago your baby didn't make very many demands, so satisfying them wasn't all that tough. But now his needs are far more complex, and at times you may feel that it's nearly impossible to react promptly and appropriately.

With so much to respond to, it's perfectly normal to worry that you're not reading your baby's signals correctly and that you're doing everything wrong. These feelings, of course, are made worse by a baby who won't stop crying (a reflection of inadequate fathering skills?) or by a dissatisfied or seemingly hostile look on the baby's face (possibly a reproach that you've made some terrible mistake).

Perhaps the best way to overcome your worries is to spend more time with the baby. The more practice you get, the better you'll be at understanding the baby's "language" and the more confident you'll be in responding.

Mom probably *wouldn't* buy us one, but you have to learn to make your own choices, Dad.

SIPRESS

Also, learn to go with your gut feelings. There's almost always more than one solution to a given problem, and you'll undoubtedly settle on a good one. Even if you make a few mistakes, they aren't likely to have any long-term effects. After all, just because your partner burps the baby over her shoulder doesn't mean you can't do it with the baby sitting on your knees.

Of course, if you're really sure you're making *serious* mistakes, ask for some help. But spending too much time analyzing things and worrying that you've done something wrong can get you into trouble. According to psychiatrist Stanley Greenspan, excessive worrying can destroy your self-confidence and lead to doing nothing at all or to adopting a hands-off attitude toward the baby. (That way, the twisted logic goes, at least you won't make any *more* mistakes.) This, of course, can have a decidedly negative effect on your baby's development—and on your development as a father.

Finally, before you toss in the towel, consider this: If you think you're having trouble reading your baby's signals, how can you be so sure that his crying and odd looks mean all the horrible, negative things you think they do?

Striking a Balance Between Work and Family

Most new fathers, writes author David Giveans, are "torn between the need to provide economically for the family and the desire to be a nurturing father." And finding the right balance between these two seemingly mutually exclusive options is something you'll be working on for the rest of your life.

As mentioned in the previous chapter (pages 85–86), most men place a high value on their family life and claim that they're willing to make sacrifices to spend more time with their children. But by six months after their children's birth, about 95 percent of new fathers are back working full-time. (Phil and Carolyn Cowan found that at the same point in time only 19 percent of women are employed full-time, and another 36 percent are working part-time.)

At first glance it seems that there's a major contradiction between what men say and what they do. But researcher Glen Palm found that the work/family trade-off isn't nearly so cut-and-dried. Many new fathers, Palm says, are "taking time off from friendships, recreation, and sleep to devote to their children, while they continue the time commitment to a full-time job."

Clearly there's something keeping fathers from spending less time at the office. One explanation, of course, is financial. Since the average working woman makes less than the average working man, if one parent is going to take time off from work, many families conclude that they can better survive the loss of the woman's salary.

Another important explanation is that in our society men and women have very different choices about the relative value of career in their lives. According to Dr. Warren Farrell, author of *Why Men Are the Way They Are,* women can choose between having a full-time career, being a full-time mother and homemaker, or some combination of the two. Men's choices, says Farrell, are a bit more limited: career, career, or career.

While this may be a bit of an exaggeration, the truth is that we simply expect men to show their love for their families by providing for them financially. "To many people, 'working mother' means conflict," says the Fatherhood Project's Jim Levine. "But 'working father' is a redundancy."

Perhaps the most interesting explanation (and my favorite) for why we keep fathers tied to their jobs and away from their families is offered by anthropologist Margaret Mead: "No developing society that needs men to leave home and do their thing for society ever allows young men in to handle or touch their newborns . . . for they know somewhere that if they did the new fathers would become so 'hooked' they would never go out and do their thing properly." Hmmmm.

Just because most fathers are trapped at the office doesn't mean that they aren't affected by what's going on at home. Radcliffe professor Rosalind Barnette found that men are just as likely as women to worry about family problems at the office. And according to researcher Joseph Pleck, 36 percent of fathers (and 37 percent of mothers) say work/family conflicts have caused them "a lot of stress." Pleck also says that "when stress occurs it has more negative consequences for men than for women."

Making Some Changes

Although you may never be able to resolve your work/family conflicts completely, there are a few ways you can maximize your time with your family, minimize your stress, and avoid trashing your career.

SCHEDULE CHANGES

"One of the conditions for men to become and stay highly involved in child-rearing is for their work hours to be and continue to be flexible," writes John Snarey. Here are a few rather painless flexible scheduling options to run by your employer:

♦ Work four ten-hour days instead of five eight-hour days.
♦ Work from 5:00 A.M. to 1:00 P.M. (or some other schedule) instead of the usual 9:00–5:00.
♦ Consider a split shift, for example, work from 8:00 A.M. to noon and from 5:00 P.M. to 9:00 P.M.

"It's your husband. The baby won't burp for him."

WORKING LESS THAN FULL-TIME

If you can afford to, you might want to consider one of the following options:

♦ Job sharing. You and another person divide up the responsibilities of the job. You would probably use the same office and desk. A typical job-share schedule might have you working two days one week and three days the next, while your workplace partner does the opposite. One warning: be very careful to negotiate a continuation of your health benefits. Many employers drop them for less-than-full-time employees.

♦ Switch to part-time, which is more or less the same as job sharing, except you probably won't have to share a desk with someone else.

♦ Become a consultant to your current employer. This can be a great way for you to get a lot of flexibility over your workday. There are also lots of tax advantages, particularly if you set up a home office (see more on this in the next section). At the very least, you'll be able to deduct auto mileage and a percentage of your phone and utility bills. But be sure to check with an accountant first; the IRS uses certain "tests" to determine whether someone is an employee or a consultant. If, for example, you go into the office every day, have a secretary, and get company benefits, you are an employee. Also, remember that if you become a consultant, you'll lose your benefit package. So be sure to build the cost of that package (or the amount you'll have to pay to replace it) into the daily or hourly rate you negotiate with your soon-to-be-former employer.

WORKING AT HOME (TELECOMMUTING)

Far too many managers believe in the importance of daily "face time" (actually being seen at the office). The truth is that face time is highly overrated and often unnecessary. In all the years I've been writing, I've worked for dozens of magazines and newspapers, most of which are several thousand miles from my home. And in most cases I've never even met my bosses.

I'm certainly the first to admit that being a writer isn't a typical job. But millions of Americans do work that doesn't require their physical presence in any particular place at any particular time (engineers, computer programmers, and just about anybody else who sits at a desk). If you're not a construction worker or a retail salesman, you might be a prime candidate for telecommuting.

If You're an Employer (or a Supervisor)

"Companies compete to woo skilled women," says *Wall Street Journal* columnist Sue Shellenbarger. "But many still assume that men will continue to work regardless of how they are treated as fathers." The ultimate responsibility for changing this Neanderthal attitude and helping men get more involved with their families rests at the top—with you.

♦ Change your own schedule. Many of your male employees will be reluctant to approach you with proposed schedule changes. So if you know someone has just become a father, raise the issue with him first. Chances are he'll be grateful.

♦ Make some changes. If you have enough employees, organize classes and support groups for new parents. Even if you don't have many employees, you can still offer free (or subsidized) on-site or near-site child care. You can also encourage your employees to take advantage of part-time, job-sharing, or flexible scheduling options. Overall, your company's policies should recognize that *all* parents (as opposed to just mothers) are responsible for their children's care and development.

♦ Don't worry about the cost. Companies with family-friendly policies find that the costs of implementing such programs are more than compensated for by increased morale and productivity, reduced absenteeism, and lower turnover. They're also a great recruiting tool.

Now don't get too excited: it's not as if you and your boss will never see each other again. Most telecommuters are out of the office only a day or two a week. And if it's going to be a workable option at all, telecommuting is something you'll have to ease yourself (and your employer) into. Like the other flexible work options discussed in this chapter, telecommuting is designed to give you more time with your family. But if you think you'll be able to save money on child care or have your baby sit on your lap while you crunch numbers, you're sorely mistaken.

If you want to give it a try, here's what you'll probably need:

♦ A computer (compatible with your employer's system)
♦ An additional phone line or two
♦ A modem
♦ A fax machine (or a send/receive fax/modem)
♦ A quiet place to set things up

Besides the convenience aspect, one of the major advantages of telecommuting is that you don't have to shave and you can work in your underwear. There are, however, a few disadvantages. Primary among them is lack of human contact: you may hate that train ride into the city or the annoying guy in your carpool, but after a few months alone in your house, you might actually miss them. You might also miss going out to lunch with your co-workers or even just bumping into them in the halls. And if you have a tendency to be obsessive about your work (as I do), you'll have to train yourself to take frequent breaks. I can't tell you how many times I've realized—at ten o'clock at night—that I haven't eaten all day and that the only time I went outside was to take the newspaper in from the porch.

Putting It All Together

No matter how you try to keep your work life separate from your family life, there's going to be plenty of spillover between the two. This isn't necessarily a bad thing. In his four-decade-long study of fathers, John Snarey found that, "contrary to the stereotype of rigid work-family trade-off, a positive, reciprocal interaction may exist between childrearing and bread-winning."

Other researchers have come to similar conclusions. "Before they became fathers, men did not appear to be conscious that home and work life often require different personal qualities," writes Phil Cowan. After becoming fathers, however, many men "described new abilities to juggle conflicting demands, make decisions, and communicate quickly and clearly both at home and at work. . . . Some described themselves as more aware of their personal relationships on the job, and more able to use some of their managerial skills in the solution of family problems."

You and Your Baby

Time for Solids

When I was a baby, the current wisdom about introducing solid foods was to do it as early as possible, often as soon as five or six weeks. One of the explanations was that babies who ate solid foods supposedly slept longer than those on bottles (almost no one was being breastfed then). Today, people are more interested in the baby's health than in whether he sleeps through the night (which eating solid food doesn't affect anyway), and most pediatricians now recommend that you delay introducing solids until your baby is anywhere from four to six months old. The recommended delay may be even longer if you or your partner has a history of food allergies (for more on food allergies, see page 112).

Even if you're tempted to start solids earlier than four to six months, resist. "Introducing solids to the younger baby can interfere with his desire to suck," says Frances Wells Burck, author of *Babysense.* "Solids may also crowd out room for milk without making up for its nutritional loss." According to Burck, there are a few other reasons to keep your baby off solids until he's truly ready:

♦ Because younger babies' digestive systems are immature, solid food—along with their nutrients—passes undigested through their systems.

♦ Babies' young kidneys have to work harder to process solid foods than they do for milk or formula.

♦ Delaying especially allergenic foods (see page 113) can reduce the likelihood of developing allergies later on.

♦ Breast- and bottle-feeding is a great opportunity for parents to cuddle with their babies, although it's nearly impossible for *you* to cuddle the baby while your partner is breastfeeding.

♦ With breasts, there's nothing to clean up; with bottles, only the bottle. But with solids, you have to wash spoons, dishes, high-chair trays, bibs, and perhaps even the floor and nearby walls.

Here's how you can tell if your baby is really ready for solids:

♦ Her weight has doubled since birth (indicating that she's getting plenty of nutrition).

♦ She's very underweight for her age (indicating that she's not getting enough nutrition).

♦ She's drinking more than a quart (32 ounces) of formula or breast milk per day.
♦ She chews on nipples (either your partner's or the bottle's) while sucking.
♦ She pays close attention when you're eating.

Remember, introducing solids does not mean that breast- or bottle-feeding will end (see pages 205–8 for information on weaning). In fact, most of your baby's nutrients will still come from milk or formula for a few more months.

Getting Started

Getting your baby to eat solid foods isn't going to happen overnight. For starters, he'll probably take a few days to get used to the strange new taste and texture. Then he's got to figure out how to move it from the front of his mouth to his throat (liquids kind of know where to go by themselves), where he can swallow it. Here's the way to do it:

♦ Your baby's first food should be a single-grain cereal (no, not Cheerios)—oatmeal, barley, or rice. For the first few days, add breast milk or formula—but *not* cow's milk—to make the cereal especially liquidy. If you're buying packaged baby cereal, get the kind that's iron fortified.
♦ Offer new foods at the beginning of the meal, when the baby is likely to be at his hungriest.
♦ Three days after you actually manage to get some cereal down the baby's throat, start adding vegetables—one at a time, three to five days apart. Make sure the baby gets a good mix of yellow (carrots, squash) and green (peas, spinach, zucchini) veggies. Many people prefer to make bananas baby's first noncereal food. The problem with bananas is that they are fairly sweet, and babies may become so fond of them that they won't be interested in any other foods you may introduce thereafter.
♦ After a week or so on vegetables, introduce the bananas and some other noncitrus fruits (again, one at a time, three to five days apart). Until he's a year old, your baby can't digest raw apples, but applesauce is okay. Hold off on the oranges for a few more months.
♦ If you absolutely must give your baby juice (see page 28 for a few reasons not to), be sure to dilute it fifty-fifty with water.
♦ When your baby is about seven months old, introduce yogurt. It's an important source of protein and can easily be mixed with other foods. Although most babies like yogurt, mine didn't, and we had to trick them into eating it by putting a blueberry (always a favorite food) at the back of the spoon.
♦ Breads and cereals (yes, Cheerios are okay now) are next.

Allergies and Intolerances:
What They Are and How to Prevent Them

Despite the claims of about 25 percent of American parents, fewer than 5 percent of children under three are truly allergic to any foods. True allergies are abnormal responses by the immune system to ingested proteins. The most common symptoms are nasal congestion, asthma, skin rashes (eczema and hives), chronic runny nose or cough, vomiting, and severe mood swings. In contrast, symptoms such as headaches, excess gas, diarrhea, or constipation are generally caused by intolerances, which are usually the result of an enzyme deficiency.

While you may be tempted to say, "What's the difference? A reaction is a reaction," the distinction between an allergy and an intolerance is critical and subtle. Allergies often begin in infancy and get progressively worse with each encounter with the offending food. Intolerances don't. Fortunately, most kids—except those allergic to peanuts and fish—usually outgrow their allergies altogether by age five. (Only about 2 percent of children over five have true food allergies.)

The consensus among pediatricians is that the way to deal with allergies and intolerances is to prevent them before they happen. Complete prevention, of course, is impossible. But here are a few things you can do to better the odds:

♦ Breastfeed your baby and withhold solid foods for at least four to six months.

♦ If your partner has a history of true allergies, she should reduce or completely eliminate high-risk foods (see page 113) while breastfeeding.

♦ Introduce only one new food at a time. That way, if your baby has a reaction, you'll know right away what caused it.

♦ After introducing a new food, wait three to five days before introducing another.

♦ If your baby has any of the negative reactions mentioned above, eliminate the food right away and call your pediatrician. He or she will probably tell you to take the baby off the food and reintroduce it in six months. By then, your baby may have built up the necessary defenses.

MOST ALLERGENIC FOODS	LEAST ALLERGENIC FOODS
♦ Egg whites	♦ Rice
♦ Wheat and yeast	♦ Oats
♦ Milk and other dairy products	♦ Barley
♦ Citrus fruits	♦ Carrots
♦ Berries	♦ Squash
♦ Tomatoes	♦ Apricots
♦ Chocolate	♦ Peaches
♦ Nuts	♦ Apples
♦ Shellfish	♦ Lamb

♦ At about one year, your baby can eat almost any kind of food, but in small pieces. Some foods, such as grapes, raw carrots, nuts, and hot dogs, can still present choking hazards.

♦ One big warning: Do not give your baby honey or corn sweeteners for at least the first year. They often contain tiny parasites that an adult's digestive system exterminates with no problem. But the baby's still-immature system won't be able to handle the chore.

I Wanna Do It Myself

When your baby is ready to feed himself, he'll let you know, usually by grabbing the spoon from your hand (babies are quicker than you'd think) or mushing around anything that's dropped on to the high-chair tray. When this happens, prepare yourself; in the course of the next few weeks, your baby will discover the joys of sticking various kinds of food in his nose and eyes, under his chin, behind his ears, and in his hair. And it won't be much longer until he learns to throw.

One way to minimize the mess is to put a large piece of plastic under the high chair; a large trash bag cut open along the side is good. But don't relax yet; your baby will soon learn to use his spoon as a catapult to launch food beyond this protective boundary. There's really nothing you can do about this, so avoid wearing your best clothes while the baby is eating.

Making Your Own

You can, of course, buy pre-prepared baby food in those tiny jars. But they're expensive and often filled with preservatives, chemicals, and other nasty stuff. Some companies, such as Earth's Best, offer organic, pesticide- and preservative-free foods. They're even more expensive.

Two Small Warnings

First, when you begin giving your baby solids, she's going to make an incredible array of faces: horror, disgust, fear, betrayal. Try not to take them personally. Your baby is probably reacting to the new and unknown and not criticizing your cooking.

Second, don't make a ton of food the first few times. You'll probably end up feeding the baby the same spoonful over and over again (you put some in her mouth, she spits it out; you scrape it off her cheek and put it in her mouth again . . .). This can be frustrating, but try to remember what comedian Dave Barry says: "Babies do not take solid food through their mouths. . . . Babies absorb solid food through their chins. You can save yourself a lot of frustrating effort if you smear the food directly on your baby's chin, rather than putting it in the baby's mouth and forcing the baby to expel it on to its chin, as so many uninformed parents do."

The solution: be patient and keep your video camera ready at all times.

By far the cheapest alternative is to make your own. After all, the major ingredient of most baby food is cooked vegetables. You can even do it in bulk. All you have to do is boil some vegetables, mash them up, and put the mash into an ice-cube tray. Whenever you need to, just pop out a cube, thaw, and serve.

A word of caution: Microwaves heat food unevenly, leaving hot spots right next to cold ones. So if you're using a microwave, make sure you stir well and test anything you're planning to give the baby.

Notes:

6 MONTHS

Gaining Confidence

What's Going On with the Baby

Physically

♦ By the end of this month she'll probably be able to sit by herself in "tripod position" (feet splayed, hands on the floor in between for balance). She may even be able to right herself if she tips over.

♦ She can turn herself from back to front or front to back at will, and may even be able to propel herself short distances (usually backward at first) by creeping or wiggling. Be prepared, though: she'll be demonstrating a lot of these new moves when you're trying to change or dress her.

♦ She can probably get herself to her hands and knees and will spend hours rocking back and forth, picking up an arm here, a leg there—all in preparation for crawling.

♦ She can clap her hands and bang two objects together. And whatever isn't being banged is sure to be in her mouth.

Intellectually

♦ With so many new things to do and learn, your baby is now awake about 12 hours a day and spends most of that time finding out about her environment by touching, holding, tasting, and shaking things. According to Frank Caplan, this is proof that "the need to learn is at least as important as pleasure-seeking in determining behavior."

♦ The idea that she is separate from other people and other objects is slowly sinking in. But she still thinks she has absolute control over all she sees or touches. As if to rub it in, she'll endlessly drop toys, dishes, and food from her high chair and revel in the way she can make you pick them up.

♦ Another way your baby demonstrates her complete power over the world and everything in it (especially you) is to cry for attention whether she needs any or not.

♦ Both these activities show that your baby is able to formulate plans and can anticipate the consequences of her actions.

Verbally

♦ She's now more regularly adding consonants to vowels and creating single-syllable "words" such as *ba, ma, la, ka, pa.*

♦ She's getting pretty good at imitating sounds and also tries—with some success—to imitate your inflections.

♦ She's getting so familiar with language that she can easily tell the difference between conversational speech and any of the other noises you make. She might, for example, laugh when you start making animal noises.

♦ She's also learning to like other sounds; music in particular will cause her to stop what she's doing and listen.

Emotionally/Socially

♦ Until this month, your baby really didn't care who fed her, changed her, played with her, or hugged her, just as long as it got done. But now, for about 50–80 percent of babies, *who* satisfies their needs is almost as important. You, your partner, and perhaps a few other very familiar people may now be the only ones your baby will allow near her without crying. This is the beginning of *stranger anxiety.*

♦ She'll wave her arms to let you know to pick her up, cling to you when you do, and cry if you take away a toy or stop playing with her.

♦ Despite all this, she's still incredibly curious in new situations, and will spend as much as ninety minutes taking in her surroundings.

♦ Her desire to imitate what you do has led to an interest in eating solid food.

What You're Going Through

Growing Up

There's nothing quite like having a kid to make you realize that you're a grown-up. It also makes you realize that besides being a son, you're also a father. That may sound like a painfully obvious thing to say, but you'd be

surprised at how many men have a hard time with the concept. After all, we've spent our whole lives looking at our fathers as fathers and at ourselves as sons.

Here's how a friend of mine describes becoming aware that he had made the transition: "One day I slipped my arm into the sleeve of my jacket and my father's hand came out the other side."

Feeling Like a Father

According to Bruce Drobeck, a large percentage of men see the fatherhood role as that of a teacher of values and skills. Until they can actually communicate with their children, these men don't quite feel that they've become fathers. And since it's hard to communicate with a helpless and essentially nonresponsive baby, caring for one doesn't seem very fatherly.

But by the time your baby is six months old, she's no longer unable to communicate. She turns her head when you call her, she gets excited when you walk into the room. And when you wrestle with her, build a tower together, or tickle her, she'll give you a smile that could melt steel—a smile that's only for you. You're starting to feel confident that your baby needs you and that you're playing an important and influential role in her young life. You're finally starting to feel like a father; and the more you and your baby interact, the more you'll feel that way.

Jealousy

"The single emotion that can be the most destructive and disruptive to your experience of fatherhood is jealousy," writes Dr. Martin Greenberg in *The Birth of a Father.*

There's certainly plenty to be jealous about, but the real question is: Whom (or what) are you jealous of? Your partner for her close relationship with the baby and the extra time she gets to spend with her? The baby for taking up more than her "fair share" of your partner's attention and for having full access to her breasts while they may be "too tender" for you to touch? The baby-sitter for being the recipient of the baby's daytime smiles and love—tokens of affection you'd rather were directed at you? Or maybe it's the baby's carefree life. The answer, of course, is: All of the above.

Like most emotions, a little jealousy goes a long way. Too much can make you feel competitive toward or resentful of your partner, the baby-sitter, even the baby. Do you feel you need more attention or emotional support from your partner? Do you need more private time with the baby? Whatever or whomever you're jealous of, it's critical to express your feelings clearly and honestly and to encourage your partner to do the same. If for some reason you feel you can't discuss your feelings on this issue with your partner, take them up with a male friend or relative. You'll be surprised at how common jealousy is. Jealousy's "potential for destruction," writes Greenberg, "lies not in having the feelings but in burying them."

Gaining Confidence

I don't remember every day of my children's childhoods, but there's one day in particular—when my older daughter was about six months old—that I recall quite clearly.

It really wasn't all that different from any other day. I gave her a bottle and dressed her. When she threw up all over her clothes, I dressed her again. Five minutes later she had an explosive bowel movement that oozed all the way up to her neck, so I cleaned her up and dressed her for the third time. Over the course of the day I probably changed five more diapers and two more outfits, gave her three bottles, calmed her from crying four times, took her in and out of the car eight times as I drove all over town doing errands, put her down for two successful naps during which I managed to do a few loads of laundry and wash the dishes. I even managed to get some writing done.

All in all, it wouldn't have been a very memorable day if it weren't for what happened at the end of it. As I sat in bed reading, I remember thinking to myself, "Damn, I'm really getting a pretty good handle on this dad stuff." The truth is that I was. And by now, you probably are too.

Things that would have had you panicking a few months ago now seem completely ordinary. You've learned to understand your baby's cues, you can predict the unpredictable, and those feelings of not being able to do things right are nearly gone. You probably feel more connected and attached to your baby than ever before. The feeling is one of confidence and stability, and signals that you've entered what some sociologists and psychologists refer to as the "honeymoon period" with your baby.

For many men, feelings of confidence as fathers lead them to feel more confident in their relationships with their partners as well. A majority of men in fatherhood researcher Bruce Linton's studies felt that their relationships with their partners had gotten "easier" and described a sensation of connection and attachment to both baby and partner—kind of "bonding as a family."

You and Your Baby

Playing Around

As your baby develops her reaching, grabbing, and shoving-things-into-her-mouth skills, she'll gradually lose interest in face-to-face play and become more focused on the objects around her (or at least the ones she can reach) and on exploring her environment.

The first, and perhaps most important, lesson your baby will learn about objects is that she can, to a certain extent, control them. Of course, this startling epiphany comes about as a complete accident: you put a rattle in her hand and after swinging her arms around for a while, she'll notice that the rattle makes some noise. But over the course of several months, your baby will learn that when she stops flailing, the rattle stops rattling and that she can—just because she wants to—get it to rattle again, and again, and again.

Your baby will learn quite a bit about objects all by herself. But if you're interested, there are a number of games you can play with your baby that, besides being fun, will encourage object awareness and perception.

REACHING GAMES

To encourage your baby to reach and to expand her horizons, try holding attractive toys just out of her reach: above her head, in front of her, to the sides. See how close you have to get the toy before she makes her move. Remember, the object here is not to tease or torture the baby, it's to have fun.

TOUCHING GAMES

Try this: Let your baby play with a small toy without letting her see it (you might want to do this in the dark or with her hands in a paper bag). Then put that toy together with several other toys she's never played with. Many babies this age will pick up the familiar toy. Although this may sound fairly easy, it isn't. You're asking your baby to use two senses—touch and vision—at the same time. If your baby isn't ready for this one, don't worry. Just try it again in a few weeks.

IF . . . THEN . . . GAMES

There are thousands of things you can do to reinforce cause-and-effect thinking. Rattles, banging games, rolling a ball back and forth, and splashing in the pool are excellent. So is blowing up your cheeks and having the baby "pop" them. Baby gyms—especially the kind that make a lot of noise when smacked—are also good, but be sure to pack them up the moment your baby starts trying to use the gym to pull herself up; they just aren't sturdy enough.

Give the Kid a Break

Don't feel that you have to entertain your baby all the time. Sure it's fun, but letting her have some time to play by herself is almost as important to her development as playing with her yourself. And don't worry; letting her play alone—as long as you're close enough to hear what she's doing and to respond quickly if she needs you—doesn't mean you're being neglectful. Quite the opposite, in fact. By giving her the opportunity to make up her own games or to practice on her own the things she does with you, you're helping her learn that she's capable of satisfying at least some of her needs by herself. You'll also be helping her build her sense of self-confidence by allowing her to decide for herself what she'll be playing with and for how long.

GOOD TOYS	BAD TOYS
◆ Blocks	◆ Anything made of foam—it's too easy to chew off pieces
◆ Dolls with easy-to-grasp limbs	
◆ Real things: phones, computer keyboards, shoes, etc.	◆ Anything small enough to swallow or that has detachable parts
◆ Toys that make different sounds and have different textures	◆ Anything that could possibly pinch the baby
◆ Musical toys	◆ Anything that runs on electricity
◆ Balls	◆ Stuffed animals and other furry things that might shed (stuffed animals that *don't* shed are fine)
◆ Sturdy books	
	◆ Toys with strings, ribbons, elastic—all potential choking hazards

OBJECT PERMANENCE

When your baby is about six or seven months old, the all-important idea that objects can exist even when they're out of sight slowly starts sinking in.

◆ Peek-a-boo and other games that involve hiding and finding things are great for developing object permanence. Peek-a-boo in particular teaches your baby an excellent lesson: when you go away, you always come back. This doesn't sound like much, but making this connection now lets her know she can count on you to be there when she needs you and will help her cope with *separation anxiety* (see pages 154–55).

◆ Object permanence develops in stages. If you're interested in seeing how, try this: Show your baby a toy. Then, while she's watching, "hide" it under a pillow. If you ask her where the toy is, she'll probably push the pillow out of the way and "find" it. But if you quickly move the toy to another hiding place when she's not looking, the baby will continue to look for it in the first hiding place.

TRACKING GAMES

Hold an object in front of the baby. When you're sure she's seen it, let it drop out of your hand. At five or six months, most babies won't follow the object down. But starting at about seven months, they'll begin to anticipate where things are going to land. When your baby has more or less mastered this skill, add an additional complication: drop a few objects and let her track them down. Then hold a helium balloon in front of her and let it go. She'll look down and be rather stunned that the balloon never lands. Let her hold the string of the balloon and experiment.

Again, if your baby doesn't respond to some, or any, of the activities suggested here, don't worry. Babies develop at very different rates, and what's "normal" for your baby may be advanced—or delayed—for your neighbor's.

Family Matters

Finding Quality Child Care

Most parents instinctively feel (and there's plenty of research to back them up) that to have one or both of them care for their baby in their own home would, in a perfect world, probably be the best child-care option. But most couples can't afford the traditional dad-goes-to-work-while-mom-stays-at-home option or the less-traditional mom-goes-to-work-while-dad-stays-at-home scenario. So chances are that, sooner or later, you'll need to consider some form of day care for your child. Here are some of the options, along with their advantages and disadvantages.

IN-HOME CARE

Unless you work at home, in-home care is probably the most convenient option for parents. You don't have to worry about day-care schedules, and your baby can stay in the environment to which he or she has become accustomed. In addition, your baby will receive plenty of one-on-one attention, and, if you stay on top of the situation, the caregiver will keep you up to date on your child's development. Finally, by remaining at home, your child will be less exposed to germs and illness.

Leaving your child alone with a stranger can be daunting and traumatic, especially the first time. On the one hand, you might be worried about whether you really know (and can trust) the caregiver. You might also be worried—as I was—that no one will be able to love or care for your child as well as you and your partner. On the other hand, you might experience what psychologist and parenting guru Dr. Lawrence Kutner calls the "natural rivalry" between parents and caregivers. "As parents, we want our children to feel close (but not too close) to the other adults in their lives. We worry that, if those attachments are too strong, they will replace us in our child's eyes."

Fortunately, no one will ever be able to replace you—or your love. But

Au Pairs

Au pairs are usually young women who come to the States on yearlong cultural exchange programs administered by the United States Information Agency (USIA). Legally, au pairs are nonresident aliens and are exempt from social security, Medicare, and unemployment taxes (see below for more on taxes and payroll).

What an au pair provides is up to forty-five hours per week of live-in child care. In exchange, you pay a weekly stipend (currently about $155) as well as airfare, insurance, an educational stipend, program support, and full room and board. On average, having an au pair will set you back about $12,000 for the full year.

You can hire an au pair through one of only eight USIA-approved placement agencies. You could hire one through a non-USIA agency, but the au pair would be subject to immediate deportation and you to a $10,000 fine.

Having an au pair can be a wonderful opportunity for you and your baby to learn about another culture. One drawback, however, is that they can stay only a year; then it's *au revoir* to one, *bonjour* to another. In addition, it's important to remember that from the young woman's perspective, being an au pair is a cultural thing. In theory she's supposed to do a lot of child care and other work, but in reality she may be far more interested in going to the mall with her new American friends or hanging out with your neighbor's teen-age son.

there are many wonderful caregivers out there who can give your baby the next best thing. You just need to know how to find them.

HOW TO FIND IN-HOME CAREGIVERS

The best ways to find in-home caregivers are:

♦ Agencies
♦ Word of mouth
♦ Bulletin boards (either caregivers respond to your ad, or you respond to theirs)

The first thing to do is to conduct thorough interviews over the phone—this will enable you to screen out the obviously unacceptable candidates (for example, the ones who are only looking for a month-long job, or those who don't drive if you need a driver). Then invite the "finalists" over to meet with you, your partner, and the baby in person. Make sure the baby and the prospective caregiver spend a few minutes together, and pay close attention to how they interact. Someone who approaches your baby cautiously and speaks to her reassuringly before picking her up is someone who understands, and cares about, your baby's feelings. And someone who strokes your baby's hair and strikes up a "conversation" is a far better choice than a person who sits rigidly with your baby on her knee.

Another good "test" for potential caregivers is to have them change your baby's diapers. Does the applicant smile or sing or try some other way to make getting changed interesting and fun for the baby, or does she seem disgusted by the whole thing? And be sure that she washes her hands when she's done.

When you've finally put together your list of finalists, get references—and check at least two (it's awkward, but absolutely essential). Ask each of the references why the baby-sitter left his or her previous jobs, and what the best and worst things about him or her were. Also, make sure to ask the prospective caregiver the questions listed below.

When you make your final choice, have the person start a few days before you return to work so you can all get to know each other, and, of course, so you can spy.

WHAT TO ASK THEM

Here are a few good questions to ask prospective in-home caregivers. You may want to add a few more from the sections on other child-care options.

- ♦ What previous child-care experience have you had (including caring for younger relatives)?
- ♦ What age children have you cared for?
- ♦ Tell us a little about your own childhood.
- ♦ What would you do if . . . ? (Give several examples of things a child might do that would require different degrees of discipline.)
- ♦ When would you hit or spank a child? (If the answer is anything other than "Never," find yourself another candidate.)
- ♦ How would you handle . . . ? (Name a couple of emergency situations, such as a gushing head wound or a broken arm.)
- ♦ Do you know baby CPR? (If not, you might want to consider paying for the caregiver to take a class.)
- ♦ What are your favorite things to do with kids?
- ♦ Do you have a driver's license?

♦ What days/hours are you available/not available? How flexible can you be if an emergency arises while we're at work?

♦ Are you a native speaker of any foreign language?

OTHER IMPORTANT ISSUES TO DISCUSS

♦ Compensation (find out the going rate by checking with other people who have caregivers) and vacation.

♦ Telephone privileges.

♦ Complete responsibilities of the job: feeding, bathing, diapering, changing clothes, reading to the baby, and so on, as well as what light housekeeping chores, if any, will be expected while the baby is sleeping.

♦ English-language skills—particularly important in case of emergency (you want someone who can accurately describe to a doctor or 911 operator what's going on).

♦ Immigration/green card status (more on this and other legal complications below).

You might want to draw up an informal contract listing all of the caregiver's responsibilities—just so there won't be any misunderstandings.

LIVE-IN HELP

Hiring a live-in caregiver is like adding a new member to the family. The process for selecting one is similar to that for finding a non-live-in caregiver, so you can use most of the questions listed above for conducting interviews. After you've made your choice, try out your new relationship on a non-live-in basis for a few weeks, just to make sure everything's going to work out to everyone's satisfaction.

To Grandmother's (or Grandfather's) House We Go

If your parents, in-laws, or other relatives live in the neighborhood, they may provide you with a convenient, loving, and low-cost child-care alternative. According to a recent survey by the U.S. Census Bureau, about 16 percent of children under five years old are being cared for by their grandparents while their parents are working—half of them in their grandparents' homes. Other relatives account for an additional 8 percent of all child-care arrangements for preschoolers.

FAMILY DAY CARE

If you can't (or don't want to, or can't afford to) have someone care for your child in your home, the next best alternative is to have your child cared for in someone else's home. Since the caregiver is usually looking after only two or three children (including yours), your baby will get the individual attention he needs as well as the opportunity to socialize with other children. And since the caregiver lives in his or her own house, personnel changes are unlikely; this gives your baby a greater sense of stability.

Be sure to ask potential family-day-care providers what kind of backup system they have to deal with vacations and illness (the provider's). Will you suddenly find yourself without child care or will your baby be cared for by another adult whom both you and your baby know?

GROUP DAY CARE

Many people—even those who can afford in-home child care—would rather use an out-of-home center. For one, a good day-care center is, as a rule, much better equipped than your home, or anyone else's for that matter, and will un-doubtedly offer your child a wider range of stimulating activities. But remem-ber, "There is absolutely no relationship between the amount of money a child-care center charges and the quality of care your baby will receive," writes Lawrence Kutner. "The best child-care centers invest in hiring and retaining the best people, not buying the most toys."

Many parents also prefer group day care because it usually offers kids more opportunities to play with one another. In the long run, most parenting experts agree that being able to play with a variety of other kids helps children become better socialized and more independent. The downside, of course, is that your child won't get as much individual attention from the adult caregivers; and since your six-month-old won't really be playing with other kids for a while longer, adult-baby contact is more important. In addition, interacting with other kids usually means interacting with their germs: children in group day care tend to get sick a lot more often than those cared for at home (whether yours or someone else's).

Where to Find Out-of-Home Caregivers

You're most likely to find out-of-home child-care facilities through word of mouth or by seeing an ad in a local parenting newspaper. Perhaps the easiest (and safest) alternative is through Child Care Aware, a nationwide campaign created to help parents identify quality child care in their communities. Contact them at 1-800-424-2246.

However you find out about a potential child-care facility, there's no substitute for checking it out for yourself in person. Here are some of the things Child Care Aware suggests you keep in mind when comparing child-care facilities:

ABOUT THE CAREGIVERS

♦ Do they seem to really like children? And do the kids seem to like them?
♦ Do they get down on each child's level to speak to the child?
♦ Are the children greeted when they arrive?
♦ Are the children's needs quickly met even when things get busy?
♦ Are the caregivers trained in CPR, first aid, and early childhood development?
♦ Are they involved in continuing education programs?
♦ Does the program keep up with children's changing interests?
♦ Will the caregivers always be ready to answer your questions?
♦ Will they tell you what your child is doing every day?
♦ Are parents' ideas welcomed? Are there ways for you to get involved if you want to?
♦ Are there enough caregivers for the number of kids? (One adult for four kids is the absolute maximum ratio you should accept; if there are two or more infants the ratio should be less.)

ABOUT THE FACILITY

♦ Is the atmosphere bright and pleasant?
♦ Is there a fenced-in outdoor play area with a variety of safe equipment?
♦ Can the caregivers see the entire playground at all times?
♦ Are there different areas for resting, quiet play, and active play?
♦ What precautions are taken to ensure that kids can be picked up only by the person you select? Do strangers have access to the center?
♦ Are there adequate safety measures to keep children away from windows, fences, and kitchen appliances and utensils (knives, ovens, stoves, household chemicals, and so forth)?

ABOUT THE PROGRAM

♦ Is there a daily balance of play time, story time, and nap time?
♦ Are the activities right for each age group?
♦ Are there enough toys and learning materials for the number of children?
♦ Are the toys clean, safe, and within reach of the children?

ABOUT OTHER THINGS

♦ Do you agree with the discipline practices?

Taxes and Government Regulations

If you hire an in-home caregiver or family day-care provider, here are some of the steps you have to take to meet IRS, INS, and Department of Labor requirements:

- Get a federal ID number (you may be able to use your social security number)
- Register with your state tax department
- Register with the Department of Labor
- Calculate payroll deductions (and, of course, deduct them)
- File quarterly reports to your state tax board
- Calculate unemployment tax
- Get a worker's compensation policy and compute the premium (usually a percentage of payroll rather than a flat fee for the year)
- Prepare W-2 and W-4 forms
- Demonstrate compliance with Immigration and Naturalization Service guidelines

If the prospect of doing all this doesn't make you want to quit your job to stay home with the baby, nothing will. There is, however, an alternative: get in touch with Alan L. Goldberg, president of NannyTax, Inc. (phone: 212-867-1776; fax: 212-867-2045). His organization takes care of all these matters and any other pesky details that may arise.

- Do you hear the sounds of happy children?
- Is the program licensed or regulated? By whom?
- Are surprise visits by parents encouraged?
- Will your child be happy there?

Try to visit each facility more than once, and after you've made your final decision, make a few unannounced visits—just to see what goes on when there aren't any parents around.

A FEW THINGS TO GET SUSPICIOUS ABOUT

- Parents are not allowed to drop in unannounced. You need to call before visiting or coming to pick up your child.
- Parents dropping off kids are not allowed into the care-giving areas.
- Your child is unhappy after several months.

♦ There seem to be new and unfamiliar caregivers almost every day.

♦ You don't get any serious response when you voice your concerns.

Finding a good child-care provider is a lengthy, agonizing process, and it's important not to give up until you're satisfied. "Half to three-quarters of parents who use daycare feel they have no choices and must settle for what they can find," writes Sue Shellenbarger, author of the Work & Family column for the *Wall Street Journal.* The result? Most infants get mediocre care. A recent study by the Work and Families Institute (WFI) found that only 8 percent of child-care facilities were considered "good quality," and 40 percent were rated "less than minimal." According to WFI's president, Ellen Galinsky, 10 to 20 percent of children "get care so poor that it risks damaging their development." So be careful.

Notes:

A Whole New Kind of Love

What's Going On with the Baby

Physically

♦ He's getting so good at sitting that he doesn't need his hands for balancing anymore. Instead, he can—and will—use them to reach for things.

♦ He can get himself to a sitting position from his stomach.

♦ He's starting to crawl, but don't be surprised if he goes backward at least some of the time, or, instead of crawling, scoots around on his bottom, using one arm to pull, the other to push.

♦ If you hold him upright, supported under the arms, he can bear some weight on his feet and will stamp and bounce up and down.

♦ He now uses his opposable thumb almost like you do, and is able to pick up what he wants confidently and quickly. He still prefers objects he can bang together and, of course, put into his mouth.

Intellectually

♦ As his brain develops, so does his ability to make associations. He recognizes the sound of your approaching footsteps and starts getting excited even before you come into his room.

♦ If confronted with blocks of different sizes, he will pick each one up, manipulate them a bit, then line them up to compare them to one another.

♦ He's so thrilled with his newfound ability to pick up and hold objects, he just can't get enough. He spends a lot of time examining objects upside down and from other angles. And if he's holding a block in one hand, he'll reach for a second one and eye a third—all at the same time.

♦ The idea that objects may exist even when he can't see them is just beginning to take shape. If he drops something, he no longer thinks it's gone forever. Instead, he'll grope around for it or stare intently at the place it disappeared from, hoping to bring it back. But if it doesn't show up within 5 to 10 seconds, he'll forget about it.

Verbally

♦ A few months ago, your baby was capable (with practice) of producing any sound that a human can produce. But since he spends all his time trying to make the sounds *you* make, he's forgetting how to make the ones you don't (like rolled Rs or the clicks of the African bush people).

♦ In English, though, your baby's babbling is shifting from single-syllable to multisyllable (*babababa, mamamama, dadadada* . . .). He's able to modulate the tone, volume, and speed of his sounds and actively tries to converse with you, vocalizing after you stop speaking and waiting for you to respond to him.

♦ Your baby's passive language skills are also improving. He now turns when he hears his own name and understands several other words.

Emotionally/Socially

♦ Although he's fascinated with objects, your baby really prefers social interactions and one-on-one activities, such as chasing and fetching.

♦ He can now tell the difference between adults and children, and may be interested in playing with (actually, alongside) kids his own age.

♦ He recognizes, and reacts differently to, positive and negative tones of voice and happy or sad facial expressions.

♦ Shyness or anxiety around strangers continues.

♦ Continuing on his mission to imitate everything you do, your baby now wants to finger-feed himself or hold his own bottle or cup.

What You're Going Through

A New and Different Kind of Love

Sooner or later, almost every writer takes a crack at trying to describe love. And for the most part, they fall short. The problem is that there are so many different kinds. The love I feel for my wife, for example, is completely different from the love I feel for my sisters, which is different from the love I feel for my parents. And none of those seems even remotely similar to the love I have for my children.

I usually describe my love for my children in fairly happy terms, but periodically I experience it in a completely different way—one that sometimes frightens me.

Here's how it happens: I'm watching one of my daughters (either one will do) play in the park, her beautiful, innocent face filled with joy. All of a sudden, out of nowhere, I begin to imagine how I would feel if something terrible were to happen to her. What if she fell and broke her neck? What if she got hit by a truck? What if she got horribly sick and died? The loss is almost palpable, and just thinking about these things is enough to depress me for the rest of the day.

And there's more. Sometimes my imagination goes a step further and I wonder what I would do if someone, anyone, tried to hurt or kidnap or kill one of my children. At the very instant that that thought pops into my head, my heart suddenly begins beating faster and so loudly I can almost hear it, my breathing quickens, and my teeth and fists clench. I haven't hit another person outside a Karate studio for more than twenty-five years. But during those brief moments when my imagination runs loose I realize that I would be perfectly capable of killing another human being with my bare hands and without a moment's hesitation.

Feeling Isolated

When my older daughter was still quite young, she and her baby-sitter spent several mornings a week at Totland, a nearby park that had become something of a Mecca for caretakers and children. Most afternoons I'd come to pick up my daughter at the park, and I'd stay for an hour or so watching her play with the other kids.

The other caregivers—almost all of whom were women—would be gathered in groups of four or five, chatting, sharing information, and learning from each other. And newcomers—as long as they were female—were quickly welcomed into these groups. But despite the nodding relationships I had developed with a few of the women, I was never made completely welcome. "It's strange being a man in this woman's place," writes David Steinberg, describing a trip to the park with his baby. "There is an easy-going exchange among the women here, yet I am outside of it. . . . Maybe it's all in my head, just me being uncomfortable about integrating this lunch counter. Whatever it is, it leaves me feeling strange and alone."

Once in a while another father would come to the park with his child, and we'd nod, smile, or raise our eyebrows at each other. We probably had much in common as fathers, shared many of the same concerns, and could have learned a lot from each other. But we didn't. Instead, we sat ten yards apart; if we ever spoke, it was about football or something equally superficial. Each of us was afraid to approach the other for fear of seeming too needy, too ignorant, or not masculine enough. What a couple of idiots.

Unfortunately, the majority of new fathers in the same situation would do exactly the same thing. "Most men," says Bruce Linton, "turn to their wives, not to other men, to help them understand their feelings about fatherhood." That approach, however, is often less than completely satisfying. Even if their wives are supportive, most men report that "there's something they are not 'getting,'" says Linton. The result is that many new fathers feel isolated; they have all sorts of concerns, worries, and feelings they don't completely understand, and they think there's no one else they can share their experience with. Fatherhood, it seems, can be a lonely business at times.

Getting Together with Other Men

One of the best ways to overcome your feelings of isolation or loneliness as a father is to join or start a fathers' group. Even in California, where there are so many support groups that there are support groups for people who belong to too many support groups, the idea of being involved in a fathers' group still sounds a little risky. But according to Doug Spangler, author of *Fatherhood: An Owner's Manual,* there are many important reasons to do it:

♦ Education. Women get a ton of parenting (and other) advice from other women: where to buy the best used children's clothes, places to take the kids on rainy days, surefire cures for illnesses, ways to soothe crying babies, finding and hiring baby-sitters. You'd be surprised how much you already know, and how much you'll be able to help other men.

♦ Perspective. It won't take long for you to learn that you're not the only father who is having the feelings or thoughts you are. Yet because each of us has a different way of looking at or doing things, you'll have plenty of unique insights to contribute to the other guys in the group.

♦ Opportunities for sharing. Like most men, you probably have a few things you just can't talk about with your wife. When those issues arise, you need a couple of guys who are—or have been—experiencing some of the same things you have.

♦ Encouragement. If you're having a tough time with something, or you need help making a decision, you'll be able to tap into the collective wisdom of other men who have made fatherhood a priority in their lives.

*"Gotta go, guys. I've had about all the male bonding
I can take for today."*

♦ Accountability. The other fathers in your group will support you, but because they're guys, they'll also let you know if you're screwing up.

Finding other fathers to join a group probably won't be easy. But if you put the word out you're sure to get some responses. Here are some likely sources of new (or existing) fathers:

♦ Your church or synagogue
♦ The hospital where your baby was born
♦ Your partner's OB/GYN
♦ Your pediatrician
♦ Leaders of mothers' groups

If you aren't comfortable joining a group (and there are plenty of us who aren't), it's still important to make regular contact with other fathers. You can do this one-on-one with another father, or, if you've got a computer, by logging on to the Internet. There are discussion groups, lists, and Web pages dealing with just about every aspect of parenting: some for both mothers and fathers, some just for fathers. Almost all of these services are available for free. There's a listing of good Internet addresses in the Resources appendix at the end of this book.

According to Bruce Linton, "A father's need for friendships with other fathers is critical to his continued development." In addition, there's plenty of research indicating that fathers who join support groups are generally happier. So don't think you can handle by yourself every fatherhood-related matter that comes up. You can't. And trying to do so will only hurt your kids and yourself.

You and Your Baby

A (Very) Brief Introduction to Discipline

"Discipline is the second most important thing you do for a child," says pediatrician T. Berry Brazelton. "Love comes first." There's no question in my mind that Brazelton is absolutely right. But before we go any further, let's clarify one thing: Discipline does *not* mean "punishment"; it means "teaching" and "setting limits."

According to pediatrician Burton White, there is absolutely no need to discipline kids under seven months. There are two main reasons for this. First, your child simply isn't capable of understanding that she's doing

"Your father and I have come to believe that incarceration is sometimes the only appropriate punishment."

something wrong. She has no idea at this point what "right" and "wrong" mean. Second, babies under about seven months have very short memories. So by the time you've disciplined the baby, she's already forgotten what she did to get you so upset.

Starting at about seven months, though, White suggests slowly beginning

Your Baby's Teeth

Although your baby's little chompers started forming when your partner was four months pregnant, they probably won't make their first appearance ("eruption" in dental lingo) until about six or seven months. And it's not at all uncommon for a child to be toothless until his first birthday. One thing you can count on, though: whenever your baby's teeth show up, they'll be followed immediately by plaque. Yes, the same stuff that your dentist has to chip off your teeth with a chisel.

It's way too early to start taking your child to a dentist, but you should use a small piece of gauze to clean each of his teeth once a day. When he's a year old, use a toothbrush with a very soft bristle. Flossing won't be necessary for a while.

TEETHING

There are two important things to know about teething. First, your baby's teeth start showing up in a fairly predictable order: first the two lower central incisors, then the two top central incisors, and then the ones on either side. Most kids will have all eight incisors by the end of their first year.

Second, teething isn't usually much fun for your baby or for anyone else nearby. Most kids experience at least some discomfort around the tooth for a few days before it breaks through the gum. For many, those pre-eruption days are marked by runny noses, loose stools, a low-grade fever, and some general crankiness.

Fortunately, teething discomfort doesn't last long and is relatively easily dealt with. Most babies respond quite well to acetominophen (ask your pediatrician how many drops to give and don't waste your time rubbing it on the baby's gums—it doesn't work). Teething rings are also helpful, especially the kind that are water filled and can be frozen, and so, for that matter are frozen bagels (although if you go the bagel route, you'll be finding crumbs all over your house for a month).

Pacifier Safety

Generally speaking, there's nothing wrong with giving your baby a pacifier. A lot of babies have a need to suck that can't be satisfied by breastfeeding or shoving their own (or even your) fingers into their mouths. And don't worry about damaging your baby's soon-to-be-dazzling smile; most dentists agree that sucking on a pacifier isn't a problem until about age four.

Thumbs, on the other hand, are a bit more problematic. First of all, because thumbs don't conform to the shape of your baby's mouth as well as pacifiers do, there's a greater chance that thumbsucking will damage your baby's teeth (although not until he's five or so). And if your baby is a constant thumbsucker, there's a chance it will have an impact on the way he speaks. Finally, most illness-causing germs get into our bodies from our hands. Need I say more?

There are, however, some potential dangers involved in using pacifiers. Here's what to do to avoid them:

♦ Nipples should be made of a single piece of nontoxic material.
♦ The shield (the part that stays on the outside of the baby's mouth) should be nondetachable and have several holes for saliva.
♦ Check the nipple for holes, tears, or other signs of wear. If you find any, replace the pacifier immediately—you don't want baby to chew off pieces and swallow them.
♦ Never, never, never tie the pacifier around your baby's neck or use string to attach the pacifier to your baby—it can pose a serious strangulation risk. But if you're tired of picking the pacifier up off the floor thirty-eight times a day, buy yourself a clip-on holder, one that detaches easily.

to set limits. Nothing rigid—just some basic guidelines to get your baby used to the idea.

The best way (in fact, it's really the only serious option at this age) to discipline and set limits for your baby is to distract him; take advantage of his short memory while you still can. So if he's gotten hold of that priceless Van Gogh you accidentally left on the floor, give him a teddy bear; and if he's making a break for the nearest busy street, pick him up and turn him around the other way. Chances are, he won't even notice. And even if he does, he'll be disappointed for only a few seconds.

Walkers

I had a walker when I was a baby and both my kids did too. But there's a lot of controversy about whether walkers are safe or not. Supposedly, 15,000 emergency room visits per year are attributed to them. This has less to do with the actual walker and more to do with falling down the stairs. So if you keep your stairs securely gated, walkers shouldn't be a problem.

Another common complaint about walkers is that babies can build up some real speed and fly around the house smacking into everything in sight—fun for them, not so fun for you. In addition, they can be a source of great frustration for the baby: he may have a hard time going over thresholds or making the transition from smooth floor to carpet; and because walkers are usually fairly wide, babies always seem to be getting stuck behind the furniture.

If you're worried, most of the potential problems can be resolved by buying a "jumper"—essentially a walker with a bouncy seat and no wheels.

Childproofing Your House

Once your baby realizes that he's able to move around by himself, his mission in life will be to locate—and make you race to—the most dangerous, life-threatening things in your home. So if you haven't already begun the never-ending process of childproofing your house, you'd better start now.

The first thing to do is get down on your hands and knees and check things out from your baby's perspective. Don't those lamp cords and speaker wires look like they'd be fun to yank on? And don't those outlets seem to be waiting for you to stick something in them?

Taking care of those enticing wires and covering up your outlets is only the beginning, so let's start with the basics.

ANYWHERE AND EVERYWHERE

- Move all your valuable items out of the baby's reach. It's not too early to try to teach him not to touch, but don't expect much compliance at so young an age.
- Bolt to the wall bookshelves and other freestanding cabinets (this is especially important if you live in earthquake country); pulling things down on top of themselves is a favorite baby suicide attempt.

- Don't hang heavy things on the stroller—it can tip over.
- Get special guards for your radiators and raise any space heaters and electric fans off the floor.
- Install a safety gate at the bottom and top of every flight of stairs. After a few months, you can move the bottom gate up a few steps to give the baby a low-risk way to practice climbing.
- Adjust your water heater temperature to 120 degrees. This will reduce the likelihood that your baby will scald himself.
- Get a fire extinguisher and put smoke alarms in every bedroom. If you want to be extra cautious, consider a carbon monoxide detector.
- If you have a two-story house (or higher), consider getting a rope escape ladder.
- Take first aid and CPR classes; they're usually offered by the local Red Cross, YMCA, or hospital.
- Put together a first aid kit (see page 140 for the ingredients).

ESPECIALLY IN THE KITCHEN

- Install safety locks on all but one of your low cabinets and drawers. Most of these locks allow the door to be opened slightly—just enough to accommodate a baby's fingers—so make sure the kind you get also keeps the door from *closing* completely as well.
- Stock the one unlocked cabinet with unbreakable pots and pans and encourage your baby to jump right in.
- Keep baby's high chair away from the walls. His strong little legs can push off the wall and knock the chair over.
- Watch out for irons and ironing boards. The cords are a hazard and the boards themselves are very easy to knock over.
- Get an oven lock and covers for your oven and stove knobs.
- Use the back burners on the stove whenever possible and keep pot handles turned toward the back of the stove.
- Try to keep the baby out of the kitchen when anyone is cooking. It's too easy to trip over him, drop or spill something on him, or accidentally smack him with something.
- Never hold your baby while you're cooking. Teaching him what steam is or how water boils may seem like a good idea, but bubbling spaghetti sauce or hot oil hurts when it splashes.
- Put mouse and insect traps in places where your baby can't get to them. Better yet, set them after he's asleep and take your kill to the taxidermist before he gets up.

What Every Good First Aid Kit Needs

- ace bandages
- acetaminophen (Tylenol) drops and tablets
- adhesive strips
- adhesive tape
- antibiotic ointment
- antiseptic ointment
- antibiotic wash
- butterfly bandages
- clean popsicle sticks (for splints)
- cleansing agent to clean wounds
- cotton balls (sterile if possible)
- cotton cloth for slings
- disposable instant ice packs
- disposable hand wipes (individual packets)
- emergency telephone numbers
- gauze rolls or pads (sterile if possible)
- mild soap
- syrup of ipecac (to induce vomiting, if necessary)
- tweezers (for splinters and the like)
- pair of clean (surgical) gloves
- scissors with rounded tip
- sterile 4 × 4-inch bandages

It's also a good idea to have an emergency treatment manual around the house. Here are a few good ones:

- *Emergency Treatment: Infants* (for kids birth–12 months), $7.95.
- *Emergency Treatment: Children* (for kids 1–9 years), $7.95.
- *Emergency Treatment: Infants, Children, and Adults* (for the whole family), $12.95. Available in English and Spanish from Mosby/EMT, 200 North La Salle Street, Chicago, IL 60601. (800) 767-5215.
- *The American Medical Association Handbook: First Aid/Emergency*, $10.00 plus $4.00 shipping and handling. Available from Random House Ordering Department, 400 Hahn Road, Westminster, MD 21157. (800) 733-3000.

- Use plastic dishes and serving bowls whenever you can—glass breaks, and, at least in my house, the shards seem to show up for weeks, no matter how well I sweep.
- Post the phone numbers of the nearest poison control agency and your pediatrician near your phone.

ESPECIALLY IN THE LIVING ROOM
- Put decals at baby height on all sliding glass doors.
- Get your plants off the floor: more than seven hundred species can cause

illness or death if eaten, including such common ones as lily of the valley, iris, and poinsettia.

♦ Pad the corners of low tables, chairs, and fireplace hearths.

♦ Make sure your fireplace screen and tools can't be pulled down or knocked over.

♦ Keep furniture away from windows. Babies will climb up whatever they can and may fall through the glass.

ESPECIALLY IN THE BEDROOM/NURSERY

♦ No homemade or antique cribs. They almost never conform to today's safety standards. Cribs with protruding corner posts are especially dangerous.

♦ Remove from the crib all mobiles and hanging toys. By five months, most kids can push themselves up on their hands and knees and can get tangled up in (and even choke on) strings.

♦ Keep the crib at least two feet away from blinds, drapes, hanging cords, or wall decorations with ribbons.

♦ Check toys for missing parts.

♦ Toy chest lids should stay up when opened (so they don't slam on tiny fingers).

♦ Don't leave dresser drawers open. From the baby's perspective, they look a lot like stairs.

♦ Keep crib items to a minimum: a sheet, a blanket, bumpers, and a few *soft* toys. Babies don't need pillows at this age and large toys or stuffed animals can be climbed on and used to escape from the crib.

♦ Don't leave your baby alone on the changing table even for a second.

ESPECIALLY IN THE BATHROOM

♦ If possible, use a gate to keep access restricted to the adults in the house.

♦ Install a toilet guard.

♦ Keep bath and shower doors closed.

♦ Never leave water standing in the bath, the sink, or even a bucket. Drowning is the third most common cause of accidental deaths among young children, and babies can drown in practically no water at all—even an inch or two.

♦ Keep medication and cosmetics high up.

♦ Make sure there's nothing your baby can climb up on to gain access to the medicine cabinet.

♦ Keep razors and hair dryers unplugged and out of reach.

♦ Never keep electrical appliances near the bathtub.

♦ Use a bath mat or stick-on safety strips to reduce the risk of slipping in the bathtub.

Perpetual Motion

What's Going On with the Baby

Physically

♦ At this stage, your baby is in motion just about every waking minute. She's an excellent crawler and will follow you around for hours.

♦ Having mastered crawling, she's now working on getting herself upright.

♦ She'll start by pulling herself up to a half-standing crouch and letting herself drop back down. Sometime in the next few weeks, though, she'll pull herself up to a complete standing position.

♦ If she's really adventurous, she'll let go with one hand or even lean against something and release both hands. Either way, she'll be shocked to discover that she can't get down.

♦ She now uses a "pincer grip" to pick things up and, because of her increased dexterity, becomes fascinated by tiny things.

♦ If she's holding a toy and sees something new, she'll drop what she's got and pick up the second. She may even retain the first toy and pick up the second with her other hand.

♦ Her finger-feeding and bottle- or cup-handling skills are improving fast.

Intellectually

♦ Your baby's increased mobility has opened a new range of possibilities for exploration and discovery. She now gets into drawers and cabinets and can empty them amazingly quickly.

♦ Her mobility also lets her get better acquainted with some of the objects she's heretofore seen only from afar. Crawling around on the floor, for example, a baby will stop underneath a chair and examine it from every possible angle. Then, writes child psychologist Selma Fraiberg, "Upon leaving the underside of the chair, he pauses to wrestle with one of the legs, gets the feel of its roundness and its slipperiness and sinks his two front teeth into it in order to sample flavor and texture. In a number of circle tours around the chair at various times in the days and weeks to come, he discovers that the various profiles he has been meeting are the several faces of one object, the object we call a chair."

♦ Now able to pick up a different object in each hand, your baby will spend a lot of time comparing the capabilities of each side of her body.

Verbally

♦ She now babbles almost constantly, using your intonation as much as she can.

♦ She can also use sounds to express different emotions.

♦ She continues to concentrate on two-syllable "words"; *b, p,* and *m* are her favorite consonants.

♦ Her name is not the only sound she knows. She'll also turn her head in response to other familiar sounds, such as a car approaching, the phone ringing, the television "speaking," and the refrigerator opening.

Emotionally/Socially

♦ With so much to keep her busy during the day, your baby may feel she doesn't have time for naps anymore. The lack of sleep, together with the frustration at not being able to do everything she wants with her body, may make her cranky.

♦ When she's in a good mood, she really wants to be included in socializing; she may crawl into the middle of a conversation, sit up, and start chattering.

♦ She can anticipate events and will, for example, wriggle her entire body when she thinks you're getting ready to play with her.

♦ She may actually be frightened by the developing idea that she and you are separate, and may cling to you even more than before. At the same time, her fear of strangers is peaking.

What You're Going Through

Learning Flexibility and Patience

Before my older daughter was born, I was incredibly anal about time; I always

*"Hey, would you kids mind holding down
the quality-time racket?"*

showed up wherever I was supposed to be exactly when I was supposed to, and I demanded the same from others. But as you now know, going on a simple trip to the store with baby in tow takes as much planning as an expedition to Mt. Everest. And getting anywhere on time is just about impossible.

It took a while, but eventually I learned that trying to be a father and Mr. Prompt at the same time just wasn't going to work. And somehow, simply accepting that fact made me a lot more forgiving of other people's lateness as well.

Interestingly, this new flexible attitude about time began to rub off on other areas of my life. Overall, since becoming a father I think I'm far more tolerant of individual differences and can more easily accept other people's limitations, as well as my own.

Whatever you're most rigid and impatient about, you can bet that your baby will figure it out and push all your buttons. That leisurely walk in the park you planned might have to be cut short when the baby panics and won't stop crying after a friendly dog licks her face. Or you might end up having to stay a few extra hours at a friend's house so as not to wake the baby if she's sleeping or, if she's awake, not to upset her nap schedule by having her fall asleep in the car on the way home.

"As soon as I get oriented to one of Dylan's patterns, he changes and a whole new pattern begins to evolve," writes David Steinberg about his son. "It's like standing up in a roller coaster. I'm finding that the more I accept this constant change, the more I can enjoy the dynamics of it, the constant growing. Dylan is deepening my sense of change as a way of life."

Not everyone, however, finds change as pleasant or as easy to accept as David Steinberg. For some, any sort of deviation from an orderly schedule, or any lack of continuity, can be very discombobulating. If you're in this category, you've got a rather Zen-like choice to make: you can bend or you can break. Babies are, almost by definition, irrational and not at all interested in your timetables. "I can't impose my rules on Dylan," writes Steinberg. "All the persuasive skills I use to get other people to do things my way are totally irrelevant to him. I am forced to accept the validity of his rules, and then to learn to integrate that with my real needs. The trick is to become less of a control freak without entirely sacrificing myself." True, true, true.

Thinking about How Involved You Are

Before I became a father, I don't think I had ever held an infant. I babysat two or three times when I was a teenager, but only when my young charges were fast asleep. And I certainly had never changed a diaper, filled a bottle, or pushed a stroller.

Whenever I imagined myself with a child of my own, she was always two or three years old and we were walking on the beach holding hands, wrestling, playing catch, telling stories. The thought that babies start off as tiny, helpless infants never really crossed my mind, and I wouldn't have been able to describe what I—or anyone else, for that matter—would do with a baby.

Most fathers-to-be know just about as much about babies as I did. But despite our ignorance, we spend a lot of time thinking about how we want to be involved with our kids. In his research, Bruce Drobeck found that although "being in-volved" means different things to different people, most men agreed that they:
♦ Don't want their partner to raise the kids alone.
♦ Don't want to be stuck in the role of the "wait-till-your-dad-comes-home" disciplinarian they may have grown up with.
♦ Want to be more open and communicative than their fathers were with them.
♦ Want to be involved with their children in a meaningful manner, from the earliest stages of development.

So how are you doing? Are you as involved with your baby as you want to be? As you planned to be? As we discussed earlier, new fathers generally do less child care than either they or their partners had predicted during pregnancy (to review the reasons why, see pages 105–6). Jay Belsky describes one study in which 74 percent of new fathers said that child care should be shared equally. But when asked whether or not they actually shared child care with their partners, only 13 percent said yes.

If you're in that 13 percent, you're probably feeling pretty proud of yourself, and you have every right to. But many new fathers—especially those who have to return to work sooner than they'd like, or have to work longer hours to bring in extra money—experience a profound sadness and longing for their families.

It's Hard to Make Up for Lost Time

There's nothing like a long day at the office to make you realize just how much you miss your baby. And when you get home, you might be tempted to try to make up for lost time by cramming as much active, physical father/baby contact as you can into the few hours before bedtime (yours or the baby's). That's a pretty tall order, and just about the only way you'll be able to fill it is to be "overly controlling, intrusive, and hyperstimulating," writes psychiatrist Stanley Greenspan. So before you start tickling and wrestling and playing with the baby, spend a few minutes reading or cuddling with her, quietly getting to know each other again—even at eight months, a day away from you is a looooong time for your baby. You'll both feel a lot better if you do.

Besides making you miss your baby, a long day at the office can also make you feel guilty about the amount of time you're away from her. Now a little guilt is probably a good thing, but far too many parents let their guilt get out of hand. And the results are not good at all. "In order to make the emotional burden easier," writes Greenspan, "they distance themselves from their children."

Although there's no practical way for you to make up for lost time, it's important that you find some middle ground between being overly controlling and distancing yourself from your baby. The best way to do that is to make sure that whenever you're with your child, you're there 100 percent. Forget the phone, forget the newspapers or the TV, forget washing the dishes, and forget eating if you can. You can do all those things after the baby goes to sleep.

He Says, She Says

Remember the story about the five blind men and the elephant? Each of them approaches an elephant and bumps into a different part—the leg, the tail, the ear, the trunk, the side—and then authoritatively describes to the others what he thinks an elephant *really* looks like. The moral of the story, of course, is that two (or more) people looking at exactly the same object or situation may see very different things.

The same moral applies when couples are asked to rate the husband's level of involvement in the home: men are more likely to be satisfied with their contribution and women are more likely to be disappointed. The problem here is not one of blindness, however. Instead, it's that men and women, according to Jay Belsky, are using different yardsticks to measure.

"A wife measures what a husband does against what she does. And because what a man does looks small . . . the woman often ends up . . . unhappy and disgruntled," writes Belsky. "The man, on the other hand, usually measures his contribution to chores against what his father did." And because he's sure to be doing more, he ends up feeling "good about himself and his contribution."

Another factor that Belsky feels contributes to a new father's tendency to overrate his participation is that ever since the baby was born, he has probably been the main, even the sole, breadwinner. And since he's been socialized to equate breadwinning with parenting, going to work "makes the 20 percent he does at home seem like 200 percent," says Belsky.

Circumstances may make it impossible for you to make any changes in the time you can spend with your family. But if you have any flexibility at all, take another look at the work/family options on pages 106–9. On his deathbed, no father ever wishes he'd spent more time at the office.

You and Your Baby

Reading

At eight to nine months of age, children who have been read to regularly can predict and anticipate actions in a familiar book and will mimic gestures and noises. So at this age it's a good idea to involve your baby more actively in the

"The weasel represents the forces of evil and the duck the forces of good, a surrogate for American air and naval superiority."

reading process. Talk about the things on the page that aren't described in the text and ask your baby a lot of identification questions. If you can, show your baby real-life examples of the objects pictured in her books.

At around ten months, your baby may be perfectly content to sit with a book and turn pages—probably two or three at a time. Don't worry if she seems not to be paying any attention to what she's "reading"; she's learning a lot about books' structure and feel. If you put a book upside down in front of your baby she'll turn it the right way. Singing, finger plays, and rhythmic bouncing while reciting nursery rhymes are still big hits.

At eleven months, your baby may be able to follow a character from page to page. This is also the age at which she may start demanding that you read specific stories or that you reread the one you just finished. Board books and sturdy flap books are great for this age.

By the time she's a year old, your baby may be able to turn the pages of her books one at a time. She will point to specific pictures you ask her to identify and may even make the correct animal sounds when you ask her, "What does a . . . say?" Be sure to respond positively every time your baby makes any attempt to speak—animal noises included.

As you've probably noticed already, reading provides you and your baby with a wonderful opportunity for close physical contact. The best position I've found (it's the one with maximum snuggle potential) is to put the baby on your lap and, with your arms around her, hold the book in front while you read over her shoulder.

When considering the next few months' reading, look for books with bright, big, well-defined illustrations, simple stories, and not too much text. Besides your baby's current favorites (which you should keep reading for as long as she's interested), you might want to check out a few of these books:

Baby Animals (and many others), Gyo Fujikawa
The Baby's Catalog, Janet Ahlberg, Allan Ahlberg
Baby's Bedtime Book, Kay Chorado
The Ball Bounced (and many others), Nancy Tafuri
Daddy, Play with Me (and many others), Shigeo Watanabe
Dressing (and many, many others), Helen Oxenbury
Goodnight Moon, Margaret Wise Brown
"More, More, More," Said the Baby: 3 Love Stories, Vera B. Williams
"Paddle," Said the Swan, Gloria Kamen
Sam's Bath (and other books in the Sam series), Barbro Lindgren
Sleepy Book, Charlotte Zolotow
Step by Step, Bruce McMillan
Spot Goes Splash (and many other Spot books), Eric Hill
Tickle; All Fall Down; Say Goodnight; Dad's Back (and many others),
    Jan Ormerod
What Sadie Sang; Sam Who Never Forgets (and others), Eve Rice
Wheels on the Bus, adapted by Paul O. Zelinsky
Who Said Meow? Maria Polushkin

CONCEPTS
The ABC Bunny, Wanda Gag
Clap Hands (and many others), Helen Oxenbury
First Words for Babies and Toddlers, Jane Salt
Ten, Nine, Eight, Molly Bang

Dealing with Stranger Anxiety

At about seven or eight months, you'll probably notice a marked change in your baby's behavior around strangers. Only a few weeks ago, you could have handed him to just about anyone and he would have greeted the new person with a huge smile. But now, if a stranger—or even someone the baby has seen before—comes anywhere near him, he'll cling tightly to you and cry. Welcome to *stranger anxiety,* your baby's first fear.

What's happening is that your baby is just beginning to figure out that he and you (and his other primary caretakers) are separate human beings. It's a scary idea, and he's simply afraid that some person he doesn't like very much might take you—and all the services you provide—away.

Stranger anxiety affects 50–80 percent of babies. It usually kicks in at around seven or eight months, but sometimes not until a year. It can last anywhere from a few weeks to six months.

Your baby is more likely to experience stranger anxiety if he's withdrawing, slow-adapting, or has low sensory threshold (see the "Temperament" section on pages 89–96). He'll be less likely to be affected if he's approaching or fast-adapting or if he's been exposed to a steady flow of new people since early infancy.

Here are a few things you can do to help your baby (and yourself) cope with stranger anxiety:

♦ If you're getting together with friends, try to do it at your own house instead of someplace else. The baby's reaction will be less dramatic in a familiar place.

♦ Hold your baby closely whenever you enter a new environment or anyplace where there are likely to be other people.

♦ When you enter a new place, don't just hand the baby off to someone he doesn't know. Let him cling to you for a while and use you as a safe haven.

♦ Warn friends, relatives, and strangers not to be offended by the baby's shyness, crying, screaming, or overall reluctance to have anything to do with them. Tell them to approach the baby as they might any other wild animal: slowly, cautiously, with a big smile, talking quietly, and perhaps even offering a toy.

♦ Be patient with your baby. Don't pressure him to go to strangers or even to be nice to them. And don't criticize him if he cries or clings to you.

♦ If you're leaving the baby with a new sitter, have her or him get to your house at least twenty minutes before you have to leave. This will (hopefully) give baby and sitter a few minutes—with you nearby—to get to know each other.

♦ If your partner stays at home with the baby while you're at work, you need to understand that your baby might lump you in with the people she considers strangers. Don't take it personally. Just follow the steps above on how strangers should approach the baby, and be patient.

Family Matters

Money

Without a doubt, money is the number one issue couples fight about. And financial squabbles are especially common during the early parenthood years, while both parents are getting settled.

Many factors contribute to quarrels over money. Here are some of the most common:

♦ **Frustration.** Women who have put their careers on hold to take a more active role at home may resent having their income (and the associated power) reduced. This goes double for men because of the still-lingering "good provider" pressures.

♦ **Your childhood.** The way you were raised can have a big impact— positive or negative—on the way you raise your own kids. If you grew up in a poor family, you may feel weird spending money on anything more than the bare necessities. Or you may feel obligated to give your child all the things you never got—at least the ones that money can buy. And if your parents were big spenders, you may be inclined to bury your baby in gifts, or you may be afraid of spoiling your child and cut way back. Whatever your overall attitude toward money, if your partner's differs considerably from yours, look out.

♦ **Differences in spending habits.** You like Cheerios and eating lunch out; your partner wants you to buy the generic brand and bring lunch from home. She makes long-distance calls in the middle of the day; you want her to wait until the rates go down.

♦ **Differences in definitions.** My wife loves to get things "half off"; the way I figure it, half off of something that costs three times more than it should is still no deal.

♦ **Gender differences.** Generally speaking, fathers and mothers have different ideas about money and what should be done with it. Fathers tend to worry about enhancing the family's long-range financial outlook and to be more concerned than mothers about savings. "Often for women new baby clothes represent a sensible economic choice because they advance another of the new mother's priorities: social presentation," says Jay Belsky. "This is the name given to her desire to present her baby—her creation—to the larger world of family and friends for admiration and praise." The big problem here is that your partner may interpret your not wanting to spend money on clothes as a sign that you don't love your baby (and, by extension, that you don't love her either).

Avoiding Money Problems, or at Least
Learning to Live with Them

- Be realistic. Having a baby can have a major impact on your financial life. Food, clothing, medical expenses, and day-care or preschool tuition all add up pretty quickly.
- Make a budget (there are plenty of good budgeting software packages, Quicken being among the best). Keep track of everything coming in and going out—even your cash expenditures.
- Hold regular monthly meetings to discuss your financial situation. Listen to each other's concerns and remember that whatever your differences, you both have the best interests of your family at heart. No blaming or yelling, and stay away from discussion-killing phrases like "You always" and "You never."
- Rearrange your priorities. Take care of the absolute necessities—food, clothing, shelter—first. If there's anything left over, start saving it for ice cream cones, vacations, private school education.
- Negotiate and compromise. You give up Cheerios and take a brown bag to lunch; she makes her long-distance calls after 11 P.M. or before 8 A.M. And remember, there are plenty of ways to cut back without having to skimp. Why pay full price for a pair of pants your child is going to outgrow in a few months when you can get a perfectly good used pair for less than three bucks?
- Make a plan. Set realistic and achievable savings goals, and make sure you're adequately insured.

Notes:

The Building Blocks of Development

What's Going On with the Baby

Physically

♦ As if recovering from the frantic developmental pace of the past two months, your baby will probably not add many new skills this month. Instead, he'll spend his time perfecting the old ones.

♦ By the end of this month he'll be such a confident crawler that he'll be able to buzz around the house grasping a block or other toy in one hand. He'll be able to crawl backward and may even make it up a flight of stairs.

♦ He easily pulls himself to an upright position and can stand (briefly) while holding your hand. He can cruise (sidestep) along furniture and walls, and when he's done, he no longer has any trouble unlocking his knees and sitting down.

♦ Now able to move his fingers separately, he has discovered that the house is filled with holes and cracks that are just big enough to accommodate his index finger.

♦ The biggest development this month (and this is pretty important) is that your baby is now coordinated enough to build a "tower" of two or three blocks (which he'll knock down immediately).

Intellectually

♦ In previous months your baby would learn a new skill and then repeat it endlessly. At this point, though, he'll begin to experiment with new ways of doing things. For example, instead of repeatedly dropping his spoon off his high-chair tray, he may start with the spoon, then drop his bowl off the other side, and finish up by tossing his cup over his shoulder.

♦ He's just beginning to come to terms with the idea that he is not the power behind everything that happens. He may, for example, bring you a wind-up toy to wind up.

♦ He's also beginning to shake his if-I-can't-see-it-it-doesn't-exist attitude, but just barely. Now if he watches you hide a toy, he will look for it. But if you hide the same toy in a second hiding place, he will continue looking in the first hiding place. In his mind, something out of his sight can exist, but only in one specific place.

♦ He's also learning about actions and their consequences. If he sees you putting on a coat, he'll know you're going outside and he may cry.

♦ As his memory gets better, you'll be able to interrupt him in the middle of an activity and he'll go back to it a few minutes later.

Verbally

♦ He's developing a distinctive "voice" in his babbling and may identify certain objects by the sound they make (*choo-choo* for train, *moo* for cow).

♦ Besides recognizing his name, your baby now understands and responds to other words and phrases, such as "No" and "Where's the baby?" He also understands and might even obey simple commands such as "Bring me my pipe."

♦ Although he's several months away from saying anything truly understandable, your baby already has a good grasp of the rhythm and sound of his native language. German researcher Angela Friederici found that even at this young age, babies are sensitive to the structure of words in their own language and can listen to a string of speech and break it down into wordlike units.

Emotionally/Socially

♦ This baby loves to play. He'll shout if he thinks you should be paying more attention to him and imitates such acts as blowing out candles, coughing, and sneezing.

♦ He may be able to get you to understand—by pointing, grunting, squealing, or bouncing up and down—that he needs something specific.

♦ Preferences are becoming more distinct, and he'll push away things (and people) he doesn't want.

♦ Perhaps a little scared of the new world he's discovering, he clings to you more than ever and cries if you leave him alone; it's the beginning of *separation anxiety* (different from the stranger anxiety of the past few months).

What You're Going Through

Feeling More Attached to Your Baby

As your baby gets older and becomes more and more responsive and interactive, your attachment to her will deepen. As we discussed earlier, however, parent-child attachments are a little bit lopsided: "It is fairly obvious," write psychologists Barbara and Philip Newman, "that soon after a child's birth the parent's attachment to the child becomes quite specific, that is, the parent would not be willing to replace his or her child with any other child of similar age."

But what the Newmans and I—and you, too—really want to know is, "At what point does the child make this kind of commitment to the *parent*?" The answer is somewhere between six and nine months. By that time, the baby has developed the mental capacity to associate you with having his needs and wants satisfied and can summon up a mental image of you to keep him company when you're not there.

But don't think that this means you needn't bother trying to establish an attachment to your baby right away. On the contrary. Attachment doesn't just happen overnight; it's a gradual process that takes months to develop, and the sooner you get started, the better. "A healthy attachment in infancy is likely to turn out a healthier adult," write the husband-wife/pediatrician-nurse team of William and Martha Sears. And the way you react and respond to your baby will have a great influence on the kind of attachment you and she eventually establish.

As you might imagine, the single most successful strategy for forming lasting, secure attachments with your children is to spend time with them one-on-one, doing everything you possibly can together, from the mundane to the exciting. "The earlier the father can feel involved with the infant," says Henry Biller, "the more likely will a strong father-child attachment develop."

Attachment theories were first developed in the 1950s by researchers John Bowlby and Mary Ainsworth, who conducted detailed studies of the interactions between several hundred parents and their children. Bowlby and Ainsworth concluded that there are two basic types of attachment: *secure*, meaning that

Attachment Basics

ATTACHMENT	TWELVE-MONTH-OLDS
Secure (about ⅔ are securely attached, but that doesn't mean they won't have any problems when they grow up)	• Are confident that their parents will be there when needed. • Know they can depend on their parents to respond to their pain, hunger, and attempts at interaction. • Readily explore their environment using parents as bases. • Don't cry much and are easy to put down after being held.
Avoidant (⅙)	• May avoid physical contact with parents. • Don't depend on parents to be secure base. • Don't expect to be responded to caringly. • Learn not to act needy no matter how much they may want to be held or loved.
Ambivalent (⅙)	• Cry a lot but don't know whether their cries will get a response. • Are afraid of being abandoned physically or emotionally. • Are worried and anxious, easily upset. • Cling to parents, teachers, other adults. • Tend to be immature and mentally scattered.

the child feels confident that the parent will respond appropriately to her needs; and *insecure*, meaning that the child is constantly afraid her needs *won't* be met by the parent. They further divided the insecure category into two subcategories: *avoidant* and *ambivalent*. (See the chart above for a more detailed explanation.)

TODDLERS	PARENTS
♦ Are independent and trusting.	♦ Respond to children sensitively and consistently.
♦ Learn early how people treat other people.	
♦ Are open to having their behavior redirected.	♦ Pick up the baby when he cries, feed him when he's hungry, hold him when he wants to be held.
♦ Mix well with all age groups.	
♦ Become social leaders.	
♦ Are curious and eager to learn.	
♦ Are less curious.	♦ Deny their (and others') feelings and needs.
♦ Are frequently distrusting.	
♦ Can be selfish, aggressive, manipulative.	♦ Believe children should be independent early.
♦ May have few friends.	♦ Don't like to cuddle with the baby or pick him up when he cries.
	♦ Can be emotionally cold.
♦ Lack self-confidence.	♦ Are wildly inconsistent and unpredictable in their parenting.
♦ May experience uncontrolled anger.	
♦ May either overreact emotionally or repress feelings.	♦ Are frequently self-involved.
♦ Are frequently less adaptable.	♦ Hope to get from the baby the love that they never had from their own parents and that they may not be able to get from each other.

Based on the information they gathered by observing babies in their first months of life, Bowlby and Ainsworth were able to predict accurately the specific behavior patterns those same babies would exhibit as they grew. Bowlby's and Aisworth's theories are just as applicable today as they were when articulated nearly fifty years ago.

In Case You Thought You Were Alone . . .

There isn't a single animal species in which the female doesn't produce the eggs. But eggs aren't worth much without the male's sperm to fertilize them. In most cases, once the eggs are laid, neither parent sticks around to watch it hatch or to meet their babies. Sometimes, though, eggs need more specialized care or they'll all perish. In these cases, one or both parents are required to pitch in. Here are just a few examples of some of the dozens of species of animals in which the father plays an important role in carrying, raising, protecting, and educating his young.

Long before the male three-spined stickleback has even met his mate, he sets to work building an attractive little house out of algae. When he's finished, he hangs out in front and makes a pass at the first female who happens by. If she's interested, the male invites her in, but, not being much of a romantic, he asks her to leave after she's laid her eggs, which he quickly fertilizes as soon as she's gone. For the next few weeks, the father guards his nest, keeping it well ventilated and repairing any damage. Until his babies hatch, the father never leaves the nest, even to eat.

Like the stickleback, the male giant water bug does everything he possibly can to attract females. If one shows any interest, he fertilizes her eggs. The female then climbs onto her lover's back and lays nearly a hundred eggs, securing each to his back with a special glue. For the next two weeks the father is completely responsible for the eggs' safety and well-being. When they finally hatch, the babies stick close to dad until they feel confident enough to swim away.

Unlike the stickleback, a cichlid (pronounced SIK-lid) doesn't need a nest. As soon as the female lays the eggs, the male scoops them up into his mouth. Because his mouth is so full, the father can't eat until the babies hatch—sometimes up to two weeks. And after they're born and can swim by themselves, dad still protects his children by carrying them in his mouth. He spits them out when it's time to eat, get some air, or just have a little fun. And when play time is over (or if danger is lurking), he sucks them back in again.

Frogs are famous for having involved fathers. After the eggs of the two-toned poison-arrow frog hatch, the tadpoles crawl onto their father's back, where they hang on with their suckerlike mouths as dad carries them through the jungle. Darwin's frogs take things one step further. Just as his tiny, jelly-covered eggs are about to hatch, the future father snaps them up with his tongue and slides them into a special pouch inside his body. The eggs hatch and the tiny tadpoles stay inside the pouch until they lose their tails and jump out of their father's mouth.

Among birds and mammals, there is a high rate of co-parenting. For example, male and female geese, gulls, pigeons, woodpeckers, and many other birds work as a team to build their homes, brood (sit on the eggs to keep them warm), and feed and protect the young after they're born. In a similar fashion, the male California mouse is responsible for bringing food into the nest and for huddling with the young to keep them warm (the babies aren't born with the ability to regulate their own body temperatures). These mice have at least two things in common with human parents. First, they are both generally monogamous. Second, the presence of an involved father has a major impact on the babies: pups weigh more, their ears and eyes open earlier, and they have a greater survival rate than pups who are separated from their fathers.

"They're hatching! Quick, Albert, get the camcorder!"

The Generational View

Like it or not, the type of attachment you establish with your baby will be influenced (not set in stone, just *influenced*) by your own attachment experience with your parents. So as you read this section, spend some time thinking about *your* childhood. Doing so may help you understand a few things about yourself and your parents. More important, it may help you avoid making some of the same mistakes with your own children that your parents made with you.

Your attachment with your child may also be influenced by your relationship with your partner. Dozens of studies confirm that the better the couple relationship, the more secure the parent-child relationship (see pages 210–12 for more on couple relationships).

The Father-Child Connection

Although the vast majority of research on attachment has focused on mothers and children, some researchers are now beginning to study father-child attachment. Their findings confirm what active, involved fathers have known in their hearts for years—that the father-child bond is no less important than the mother-child bond. Here's what the experts have to say:

♦ Researcher Frank Pedersen and his colleagues found that the more actively involved a six-month-old baby has been with his father, the higher the baby's scores on mental and motor development tests.

♦ Fatherhood pioneer Ross Parke found that "the more fathers were involved in the everyday repetitive aspects of caring for infants (bathing, feeding, dressing, and diapering), the more socially responsible the babies were and the better able they were in handling stressful situations."

♦ Researcher Norma Radin found that greater father involvement leads to increased performance in math. She also found that active fathering contributed to better social adjustment and competence, to children's perception that they were masters of their own fates, and to a higher mental age on verbal intelligence tests.

There are also factors that may interfere with father-child attachments, and researcher Glen Palm has identified several of them:

♦ Many fathers experience some tension in their relationships with their children because they feel excluded by the mother-infant bond, or because they feel that they have to compete with their partners to form a relationship with the child. Others say it's hard to form a close relationship because they feel they are unable to comfort their children adequately.

"Really, Howard! You're just like your father."

A lot of these fathers were able to form close attachments only after their children were weaned.

♦ Fathers who have to be away from home a lot during the week find that "re-attaching" with the kids on the weekends takes a lot of time and energy.

♦ Temperament. No matter how much you love your child, you'll find it easier to attach to an "easy" child than to a "difficult" one. (See pages 89–96 for more on temperament.)

♦ A small but significant percentage of fathers feel that their in-laws are overprotective of their adult daughters and get in the way too much.

♦ There is a glaring lack of information and support for new fathers.

You and Your Baby

Playing Around . . . Again

For the first seven or eight months of your baby's life, he had to be content with staring at things from across the room and waiting for you to bring them to him. But now that he's mobile, he's going to try to make up for lost time. He's incredibly curious about his world, and no obstacle can stand between him and something to touch, squeeze, gum, or grab. (If your baby *isn't* very curious, however, let your pediatrician know. But don't be alarmed if you catch the baby staring off into space once in a while. According to Burton White, babies this age spend about 20 percent of their waking time soaking up information visually.)

Although our society doesn't value play nearly as highly as some other parent-child pastimes such as feeding and diaper changing, it is, neverthe-less, critical to your baby's development. "Many children who do not have much chance to play and who are only infrequently played with suffer severe intellectual arrest or setbacks," writes developmental psychologist Bruno Bettelheim.

One of your major goals should be to expose your baby to the most varied, enriching play environment possible. But perhaps even more important is your basic philosophy about play. "Parents' inner attitudes always have a strong impact on their children," says Bettelheim. "So the way parents feel about play, the importance they give it or their lack of interest in it, is never lost on their child. Only when parents give play not just respect and tolerance but also their personal interest, will the child's play experience provide a solid basis upon which he can develop his relation to them and further to the world."

Brain Builders

These games and exercises can stimulate your baby's capacity to use different skills at the same time (seeing, hearing, thinking, and remembering,
for example):

- ◆ Get two toys that are nearly identical except that they react in different ways
  (one might need to be squeezed to make noise, the other shaken). Let the baby
  play with one of them for a few minutes, then switch. Did he get confused?
- ◆ Ring a bell, squeeze a toy, or shake a rattle. When the baby looks to see
  what made the sound, put the toy into a group of things he's familiar with.
  Will he go for the one that made the noise or will he get sidetracked by
  the other toys?
- ◆ More hiding games. A few months ago you discovered that if you hid a toy
  under a pillow or towel, your baby would push the obstacle out of the way

Vive la Différence!

As we've discussed earlier, fathers and mothers generally have distinctive but complementary styles of playing with their children: fathers
tend to be more physical; mothers, less. But besides the physical nature
of play, there are some other male-female differences you should be
able to see now.

Fathers tend to encourage their children to do things for themselves,
take more risks, and experience the consequences of their actions.
Mothers, in contrast, tend to want to spare their children disappointment, be more protective of them, and steer clear of encouraging
risk-taking.

To see how these differences might play out, imagine that your baby
is building a tower that is just about to collapse. You'll probably let the
tower fall, hoping your baby will learn from his mistakes. Your partner,
though, will probably steady the tower as it teeters.

Many researchers have found that the differences in father-child
and mother-child play styles can have a significant impact on the child.
"There were indications that children's intellectual functioning was
stimulated more in families with high father involvement," writes researcher Norma Radin. "We attribute this effect to the fact that fathers
appear to have a different way of interacting with children; they tend to
be more physical, more provocative, and less stereotyped in their play
behavior than mothers."

to "find" the toy (see page 121). Now that he's a little older and more sophisticated, you can up the ante a little by hiding an interesting toy under three or four towels. The look on his face when he pulls the first towel off and doesn't see what he was expecting will be priceless. Until he's about a year old, he'll probably get confused by the extra obstacles and forget what he was looking for in the first place.

♦ Imitating and pretend games. According to Bettelheim, engaging in this type of activity is an important developmental milestone. When our children imitate us, they're trying to figure out who we are and what we're doing. "When they imitate an older sibling or friend, they're not only trying to understand them, but they're figuring out what it's like to be older," he writes. When playing with blocks, for example, be sure to include some nonblock things such as people, cars, trucks, animals.

♦ Show him that objects can have more than one function. Envelopes, for example, can be shredded or used to contain other things.

♦ Encourage him to use tools. For example, tie a string around a toy that is well out of reach. Will he crawl to get the toy or will he pull the string to bring it closer? What happens if you demonstrate what to do? A word of caution: once your baby has mastered the idea that there are new and exciting ways to get hold of things, watch out for low-hanging tablecloths and other dangling stuff.

Exercises for the Major Muscle Groups

It's taken a while, but your baby is finally getting around to discovering that he has control over his feet. And over the next few months, he'll be making more and more use of his feet by learning to walk. He'll do this all by himself, of course, but helping him build up his muscles and coordination can be great fun for both of you:

♦ Put some toys near his feet and see if he'll kick them.

♦ Roll a ball far enough out of your baby's reach so he has to crawl to get it.

♦ Supervised stair climbing is great. But stay nearby and be extremely careful. This is a good time to start teaching your baby to come down stairs backward. But be prepared to demonstrate yourself and to physically turn your baby around a few dozen times a day.

♦ Play alternating chasing games: you chase him; he chases you. At the end, "reward" him with a big hug and—if he doesn't protest—a little wrestling. Besides being fun, these kinds of games teach your baby a valuable lesson: when you go away, you always come back. The more that idea is reinforced, the less he'll be impacted by separation anxiety (see pages 154–55).

Crawling

Although you may be in a hurry to see your baby walk, be patient. Crawling (which includes just about any type of forward movement, such as slithering, "hopping" along on the butt, or "rowing" forward with one leg) is a major developmental stage, and you should encourage your baby to do it as much as possible. There's also some evidence that makes a connection between crawling and later proficiency in math and sciences. Kids who don't crawl apparently don't do as well in those fields.

Getting Those Little Hands and Eyes to Work Together

There are plenty of activities you and your baby can do that stimulate hand-eye coordination:

- Puzzles. The best ones for this age are made of wood, have a separate hole for each piece, and a peg for easy lifting.
- Nesting and stacking toys. These help improve gentle placement skills.
- Things to crush, tear, or crinkle—the noisier the better.
- Weave some string between baby's fingers or tape two of his fingers together. Can he "free" himself?
- Stock your bathtub with toys that squirt or spin.
- Get toys that can be used in the bathtub or a sandbox to pour stuff back and forth. Measuring cups and spoons are also good.
- When you're shopping, have the baby help you put things in the grocery cart.
- If you're brave, let the baby change channels on your stereo or TV (supervised, of course).
- Play hand-clapping games.

More Experiments from the Land of Consequences

The idea that different actions produce different effects is one that can't be reinforced often enough. Here are a few ways that are especially appropriate for your nine-to-twelve-month-old.

- Jack-in-the-boxes—especially the kind with four or five doors, each opened by a push, twist, poke, or some other action. These are also good for hand-eye coordination. Be cautious the first few times, though; some babies may be frightened.
- Balls are a big hit. They roll, they bounce off things, they can knock over other things. For your baby's protection (and to reduce the chance of breaking your good dishes) make sure the balls you use are soft.

The Building Blocks of Development

There are literally dozens of cutting-edge, high-tech (and expensive) toys and games that claim to be essential to your baby's physical and mental development. Some are worthwhile, others aren't. But there's one toy— just about the least cutting-edge, lowest-tech, cheapest thing going— that truly is an essential part of every nursery: blocks. Here's why:

♦ They help your baby develop hand-eye coordination as well as grasping and releasing skills.

♦ They teach your baby all about patterns, sizes, categories (big ones with the big ones, little ones with the little ones); gravity, balance, and structure. These brief lessons in math and physics lay the foundation for your baby's later understanding of how the world works.

♦ They teach good thinking skills. "Taken from a psychological viewpoint," wrote Albert Einstein, "this combinatory play [erector sets, blocks, puzzles] seems to be the essential feature in productive thought—before there is any connection with logical construction in words or other kinds of signs which can be communicated to others."

♦ They can help babies grasp the difference between things they have control over and things they don't. "In building a tower, a child has had to deal with the laws of gravity, size, balance, etc.—laws he cannot control," says Bruno Bettelheim. "And when he knocks the tower down, he is trying to regain control over the situation."

♦ They teach perseverance. Building a tower—or anything else—out of blocks can be an excruciatingly frustrating experience for a baby. But along the way, he'll learn that if he keeps working on something long enough, he'll eventually succeed.

♦ Pots, pans, xylophones, or anything else the baby can bang on. He'll learn that different things make different noises when smacked and that hitting something hard sounds different from hitting something soft.

♦ Doors (and anything else with a hinge)—provided you're there to make sure no one gets pinched. Books operate on the same basic principle. (If you've been reading to your baby lately, you've probably noticed that he's more interested in turning the pages than in looking at what's on them.)

The bigger your baby's world gets, the more interested he'll become in objects and the less interested in you. And why not? After all, you always

> ### Success and Failure
> Whatever your baby is doing, be sure to praise his *efforts* as well as his *accomplishment*. Kids need to learn that trying to do something can often be just as important as actually doing it. Confining your praise and happiness only to successful completion of a project can make your baby less likely to take risks or try new things for fear of failing.

seem to be around, but one of those exciting new toys might disappear before he gets a chance to grab it.

Giving up the number one position in your baby's heart and mind can be tough on the ego, especially if you're being replaced by a stuffed animal or a toy car. But instead of pouting, take a more aggressive, if-you-can't-beat-'em-join-'em attitude: if you're having trouble keeping your baby interested in playing with you, use a toy to get his attention. But don't be in a hurry; wait until the baby has begun to lose interest in whatever (or whomever) he's playing with before replacing it with something new.

Family Matters

The Division of Labor
About 90 percent of new parents experience an increase in stress after their babies are born. And the number one stressor—by a huge margin—is the division of labor in the home.

Oh, How Much Work Could a Baby Really Be?
Before your baby was born, you and your partner probably anticipated that having a baby would increase the amount of household work you'd both have to do. But I'll bet you were *way* off on your estimates.

Psychologist Jay Belsky found that for most new parents, dishwashing increased from once or twice a day to four times, laundry from one load a week to four or five, shopping from one trip per week to three, meal preparation from two times a day to four, and household cleaning from once a week to once a day.

And that's just the nonbaby areas of your life. When you factor in all the baby-related stuff, things really start to get out of control. "On average, a baby needs to be diapered six or seven times and bathed two or three times per day, soothed two or three times per night and often as many as five times per day,"

writes Belsky. In addition, the baby's helplessness makes just about every task, from going to the bank to getting dressed in the morning, take five times longer than it used to.

One woman in Belsky's studies summed up the discrepancy between her prebirth workload estimate and the postbirth reality as essentially the difference between "watching a tornado on TV and having one actually blow the roof off your house."

And Who's Going to Do It?

Another thing you and your partner may have agreed upon before your baby was born was that you'd both be sharing responsibility for all the extra work the baby would require. That was a good thing: the more equitably domestic tasks are divided up, the happier couples are with their marriages. Unfortunately, though, you were most likely wrong about this one too.

"Women ended up doing more of the housework than before they were mothers," write Phil and Carolyn Cowan. "And men did less of the baby care than they or their wives predicted." Researcher Ross Parke confirmed these findings: "The birth of a baby seems to bring even egalitarian parents back to traditional roles," he writes. "There was a marked return to the customary division of labor for a variety of functions."

Everyone Knows that Women Do More Around the House, Right?

It seems that every few months or so there's a new study telling us that although women have dramatically increased the hours they work outside the home, men have barely changed the number of hours they spend working *inside*. The most widely quoted figure for men's contribution to child care, for example, is twelve minutes a day.

Pretty incriminating, eh? Well, it's not nearly as bad as it sounds. The twelve-minutes-a-day figure comes from data analyzed by Arlie Hochschild in her book *The Second Shift: Working Parents and the Revolution at Home.* And to call Hochschild's conclusions "flawed" would be charitable. Here's why:

♦ Hochschild based her findings on data gathered in 1965, although there was much more recent, and accurate, data available.

♦ When tallying *men's* hours, Hochschild "neglected" to include weekends, times when men are more likely to be actively involved with their kids.

♦ She also didn't include the hours men spend playing with their kids as child care. So if your partner is cooking dinner and you're playing with the baby, her hours are counted as household work, yours aren't. Doesn't seem very fair, does it?

♦ Even if she had counted weekends and playtime, Hochschild failed to make a distinction between *accessibility* (being on duty and available) and *engagement* (active involvement with a child). Most kids don't need or want to be entertained every second of the day, but an adult still needs to be around.

Here's what happens to Hochschild's twelve minutes a day when her errors of omission are corrected:

♦ Researchers McBride and Mills found that fathers were *accessible* an average of 4.9 hours per day on weekdays and 9.8 hours per day on Saturday and Sunday.

♦ McBride and Mills found that fathers were *engaged* with their children

an average of 1.9 hours on weekdays and 6.5 hours per day on Saturday
and Sunday.

♦ In the 1960s and 1970s fathers spent one-third as much time engaged
with and half as much time accessible to their children as their partners.
These numbers went way up in the 1980s and 1990s, to 40 percent as
much time engaged and two-thirds as much time accessible. One study
found that fathers were engaged 83 percent as much as mothers and
accessible 82 percent as much as mothers.

That's a very different story. Of course, researchers can come up with
statistics to back up just about any claim. Still, no matter how you crunch the
division-of-labor numbers, the bottom line is that women do a greater share
of the household and child-related work.

What's important to remember, though, is that in most cases this inequity
is *not* a function of men's lack of interest in their families. Phil and Carolyn
Cowan have identified five significant barriers that prevent men from taking
on a completely equal role in the home:

♦ Both men and women can't seem to shake the age-old idea that child-
rearing is women's work and that breadwinning is men's work. Many men,
therefore, are afraid of committing career suicide by openly expressing a
desire to spend more time with the family and less at work.

♦ Mothers step in quickly to take over when either the father or the baby
looks a little uneasy. At the same time, men—who hate feeling incompetent and who expect their wives to be competent with babies right from the
start—are all too glad to hand over the baby to the "expert." Jay Belsky
adds that "a woman's significant biological investment in the child can
make her so critical of her husband's parenting that, without intending to,
she drives him away." As a result, says Belsky, "men who find themselves
continually criticized for their inadequate diapering, bathing, and dressing
skills . . . feel humiliated and often conclude that the best (and safest)
policy to adopt vis-à-vis child-care chores is a hands-off policy."

♦ The roles available to men are considered second-rate and discourage male
involvement. As discussed on pages 86–88, feeding the baby—something
women generally have a lock on—is considered the most important task,
whereas soothing the baby and changing her diapers—tasks available to
men—don't seem nearly as important.

♦ The more men attempt to take an active role in the care of their children,
the more mixed or negative feedback they receive from their own parents.
During my first few years as a father, my own parents, for example, would

wonder—just loud enough for me to hear—when I'd be going back to work, or whether taking so much time off would have a negative effect on my career.

♦ The economics of the workplace and the lack of quality child care encourage fathers to work and mothers to stay home while the children are young.

The Cowans recognize that some men are willing to buck the traditional roles and do whatever it takes to get more involved. "Unfortunately, they are swimming upstream," write the Cowans, "fighting off a formidable array of forces as they try to make their way forward."

As a result, far too often *both* parents give up and adopt a more traditional division of labor. That, in turn, can lead to a decline in marital satisfaction.

Notes:

Forming an Identity

What's Going On with the Baby

Physically

♦ Unless you have a very active baby, the slowdown in motor learning that began last month will continue this month, says Frank Caplan. But don't be deceived: she's "really gathering strength to carry herself through that big step of walking."

♦ She may be able to get herself to a standing position from a crawl and, once upright, can stand with little support.

♦ She can "cruise" (sidestep while holding on to something) just about every-where, and if you hold both her hands, she'll walk and walk and walk.

♦ She's getting to be a fairly confident climber as well, getting up and down from couches and chairs almost without fear.

♦ She's also getting much better at manipulating her hands now, and can grasp two objects in one hand.

♦ She is beginning to discover that each side of her body can be used differently. And she may even be exhibiting an early "handedness" preference. She can, for example, use one hand for picking up and manipulating toys, the other for holding.

♦ If both hands are full, she may put down one object in order to pick up a third.

♦ Although she's quite graceful in her grasping, her releasing is still fairly clumsy.

Intellectually

♦ Although she still isn't completely convinced that things she can't see do exist, she's starting to suspect as much. This month, she'll look for a toy she sees you hide. If she's seen you move the toy to a second hiding place, she'll look for it there as well.

♦ She now understands that objects of different sizes need to be treated differently. She'll approach small objects with her fingers, but large ones with both hands.

♦ She's also intrigued by the idea that objects can exist for several reasons at the same time (they have properties as well as functions). Paper, for example, can be chewed, crumpled, and torn. And crayons can be held, eaten, and, best of all, used to scribble on things. This ability enables the baby to organize things into two categories ("things I can chew on" and "things that are too big to get into my mouth")—a realization that gives her a bit of control and predictability in her life.

♦ As her memory improves, she's getting more persistent. It's harder to distract her from whatever she's doing, and, if you manage to turn her attention to something else, she'll go right back to her original activity as soon as you quit bugging her.

♦ She's now capable of *symbolic thinking* (associating something you can see with something you can't). For example, a few months ago, your baby would probably cry when seeing the nurses at her pediatrician's office. She associated nurses with shots. But now she may recognize the doctor's office from the street and will start crying as soon as you pull into the parking lot.

Verbally

♦ Although she's been saying "dada" and "mama" for a while, she really didn't know what those words meant. But now "dada," "mama," "bye-bye," "no," and possibly a few others have a definite meaning that she uses deliberately.

♦ She now understands what she hears and may actually cooperate (but probably not in front of friends you're trying to impress) in a game of Identify the Baby's Body Part ("Where's your belly button?").

♦ She's also able to combine words and gestures: a head shake with "no," a hand wave with "bye-bye."

♦ She listens actively to adult conversation and will frequently butt in with a few "words" of her own.

Emotionally/Socially

♦ With physical development on hold for this month, says Frank Caplan, your baby is spending most of her energy on social and personal growth.

♦ Her mimicking skills are growing by leaps and bounds, and she'll now try to imitate just about everything you do: rubbing her hands together under running water, saying "brr" and shivering after getting out of the bath, and talking on the phone.

♦ When she cries (which she does much less frequently than a few months ago), it's less to get you to come running and more out of fear—of unfamiliar places or things, or of separation from you.

♦ She's becoming more sensitive to your emotions and is better able to express her own. If you're happy, she will be too. But if you scold her, she'll pout; if you do something she doesn't like, she's capable of genuine anger; and if you leave her alone for too long (only she knows how long that is), she may "punish" you by clinging and crying at the same time.

What You're Going Through

Feeling Irreplaceable

You've been a father for most of a year now, and, as we briefly discussed a few months ago (pages 118–19), you should be feeling pretty good about your fathering skills. If you're lucky, your partner, your friends, and your relatives have been telling you what a great father you are. But there's one person whose opinion of your abilities probably means more to you than anyone else's: the baby.

As a grown man, you'd think you wouldn't need to have your ego stroked by a baby. But the fact is that there is absolutely nothing in the world that will ever make you feel better, more powerful, or more loved than the feeling of being needed by your own child. "In the family, children send a message that you are really irreplaceable—no one has the meaning and value to your child that you do," write Barbara and Philip Newman. "The feeling that your life has meaning because of your role as a parent makes an important contribution to your sense of psychological well-being."

A Sense of Fulfillment

If feeling needed and appreciated by your boss and co-workers can give you a sense of self-worth and security at the office, feeling needed and appreciated as a father has the same result at home. In fact, nearly half the men in Bruce

*"I've never once demanded respect from you simply because
I'm your father. You should respect me for that."*

Drobeck's studies described fatherhood "as giving them more of a sense of
fulfillment and/or purpose in their lives."

For some, becoming a father was the achievement of their fondest dreams
and long-term goals. One man said, "I finally feel like I'm where I want to be
and doing what I want to be doing." Another added that having a baby "kind
of puts a reason to everything."

A New Kind of Feeling Left Out, or Mr. Baby's Father

It's hard for any father to discuss his children objectively, but you're just
going to have to take me at my word when I tell you that my older daughter
has always been exceptionally well behaved, good-tempered, and social
(my younger is pretty much the same, but this story's not about her). From
the time she was just a few months old, people would stop me on the street to
tell me how gorgeous and engaging she was. Even in France, the Parisians,
who I'm convinced share W. C. Fields's legendary love for children (he pre-
ferred them fried), were enraptured by her easy smile and made special
trips across the Champs Elysées to tickle her under the chin.

Having a baby who attracts this kind of attention (and we all do, of course) has some interesting side effects. The most common is the feeling of being completely ignored by the people who come over to gawk at your baby. This can be especially disconcerting if you actually want to meet the people who don't seem to have noticed that you're alive.

A few years ago I had a rather intense exposure to these feelings while visiting the set of *The Linguini Incident,* a movie written by one of my sisters and starring David Bowie and Roseanna Arquette. My sister had written a small scene for my wife, my daughter, and me, and the three of us had flown to L.A. for our fifteen minutes of celluloid fame.

Over the course of our twelve hours on the set, Roseanna Arquette must have taken my daughter away from me ten times, each time muttering under her breath, "Oh, my womb, my aching womb." We hardly saw our daughter all day.

At nearly midnight, we finally finished shooting, and Roseanna began saying her good-byes. She hugged the director and then came over to the table my wife, baby, and I were sitting at. Again, she took my daughter out of my arms, told her that she'd miss her, that she'd been a great little baby, that she was the best, the cutest . . . all the time kissing and kissing her. After about two minutes, Roseanna handed my baby back, said a flat "Goodnight" to me and left.

There is a strange, if false, sense of closeness that one establishes with someone who has held one's child. Roseanna had held my baby for hours, she'd told me about her womb, and I felt that we'd shared something that day— forged a kind of bond. So when I didn't get a goodnight kiss, I felt slighted.

A few months later, at the preview screening of the movie, I approached Roseanna to say hi. She gave me an icy stare and walked away. But a few minutes later she was back, smiling almost apologetically, "Oh, you're that incredibly gorgeous baby's father, aren't you?" she said. "How is she?"

You and Your Baby

Exposing Your Child to Music

By the time your baby started babbling verbally, she had already been babbling *musically* for several months—cooing happily, adjusting her pitch up or down to match yours. You'd sing or coo back and the two of you would have a little "duet."

For your baby, there is little if any difference between musical and verbal babbling. But for most parents, the difference is enormous. And the minute parents get even the slightest hint that their babies are beginning to understand language, the cooing and singing stops and they focus their attention on developing the baby's verbal skills. "Consequently," says Ken Guilmartin, president of Center for Music and Young Children, "the singing form is not reinforced and becomes developmentally delayed, or even atrophies completely."

Even if you and your partner don't have any particular musical talent, there's no reason why you can't stimulate your baby's musical potential. Now before you protest that you can't carry a tune to save your life, keep in mind that "potential" and "achievement" are *not* the same thing. Unfortunately, this is a distinction that far too many parents fail to make. And the result, says music education researcher Edwin Gordon, "can be fatal to a child's music development."

According to Gordon, every child is born with at least some musical aptitude: 68 percent have perfectly average aptitude; 16 percent well above; and 16 percent well below. "Just as there are no children without intelligence," he says, "there are no children without musical aptitude."

Good, bad, or indifferent, your baby's musical aptitude is greatly affected by the environment you provide. Even if you're so tone deaf that you're embarrassed to sing in the shower, you can easily provide your baby with a rich musical atmosphere—and you'll probably enjoy yourself in the process. Here's how:

♦ As you started when your baby was three months old (see pages 75–76), continue exposing her to a wide variety of musical styles. But now try to choose recordings that have frequent changes in rhythm, tempo, and dynamics (loudness/softness). At ten months your baby's attention span is still quite short and these contrasts will hold her interest longer and more easily, says Guilmartin.

♦ Never force your baby to listen to music. Your goal here is not to teach her (just like you won't be teaching her how to speak, crawl, or walk); rather, it is to guide and encourage her and let her develop at a natural pace.

♦ Don't turn off the music if the baby doesn't seem to be paying any attention. "There is little doubt that young children derive as much from listening to music when they appear not to be paying attention as when they appear to be paying attention," says Dr. Gordon.

♦ Try to avoid songs with words. Because your baby is rapidly developing her language skills, she may pay more attention to the words than to the music.

♦ Sing. Whenever and wherever you can. And don't worry about being in tune—your baby doesn't care. As above, use nonsense syllables—dum-dee-dum kinds of things—instead of real words.

♦ Listen to music *you* like. Your baby will be paying close attention to the way you react to the music and will know if you've selected some "good-for-you" piece that you hate.

♦ Watch your baby's reaction to the music. She's moving much more actively than a few months ago. Her arm and leg movements may seem (to adults, anyway) to have no connection to the music, but they are actually internally rhythmic.

♦ Be patient. "The process of learning music is much the same as the process of learning language," write Gordon and his associates Richard Grunow and Christopher Azzara. Here are the steps they've identified:

◊ Listening. From birth (and before), you absorbed the rhythm and inflections of your language—without any expectation of response.

◊ Imitating. You weren't too successful at first, but you were encouraged to babble even though no one understood a single "word" you said.

◊ Thinking (understanding). As you got more proficient with language, you were able to decipher the muddle of sounds coming out of people's mouths into meaningful words and phrases.

◊ Improvising. You made up your own words and phrases and sometimes other people actually understood them.

◊ Reading and writing. But not until you'd been listening, imitating, improvising, and thinking for more than five years.

Don't try to mess with the order—it's set in stone. If your parents had insisted on trying to teach you to read before you could speak, you might never have learned to do either.

Your Role in Molding Your Kids' Sexual Identity

Everyone knows that little girls are sugar and spice and all that's nice, while little boys are frogs and snails and puppy-dogs' tails, right? Well, as with most stereotypes, there is, at the core, a kernel of truth there: girls and boys *are* different and they *do* seem to behave differently, even in early infancy. Girls tend to respond to sights and sounds earlier and more intensively than boys, and they also learn to talk earlier. Boys tend to cry more and are somewhat more physical and aggressive. But what accounts for these differences—biology (nature) or the way boys and girls are treated by their parents (nurture)?

Without going into all the gory details of the debate, suffice it to say that the generally accepted view is that "sex differences in infant behavior are more a function of differential treatment than of innate biological predispositions," writes psychologist Henry Biller. "Parents may exaggerate relatively minor sex differences by talking to their girls more and handling their boys more vigorously."

Well, that was easy. But here's a much more provocative question: are the differences we see in boys' and girls' behavior—however they got there— real, or are we just imagining them?

Researchers John and Sandra Condry showed a group of more than two hundred adults a videotape of a nine-month-old baby playing. Half were told that they were watching a boy, half that they were watching a girl. Although everyone was viewing the exact same tape, the descriptions the two groups gave of the baby's behavior were startlingly different. The group that was watching a "boy" saw more pleasure and less fear in the baby's behavior than the group that was watching a "girl." And when the baby displayed negative emotions, the boy group saw anger; the girl group saw fear.

So do these imagined differences affect the way adults interact with children? The Condrys think so. "It seems reasonable to assume," they write, "that a child who is thought to be afraid is held and cuddled more than a child who is thought to be angry."

Other researchers have confirmed that adults do indeed behave differently with (perceived) boys than with (perceived) girls. Hannah Frisch conducted essentially the same experiment as the Condrys, except that in hers the adults actually played one-on-one with two different children. One time the adults were told they were playing with a boy, one time with a girl. "The general picture which emerges," writes Frisch, "is one in which adults are playing in masculine ways with children whom they think are boys and in feminine ways with children whom they think are girls."

In another study, Beverly Fagot found that by treating boys and girls differently adults may inadvertently reinforce sex stereotypes. For example, parents tend to react more positively to their daughters' attempts to communicate and more negatively to similar attempts by their sons, thus "confirming" that girls are more verbal than boys. Parents also react more positively when their sons engage in physical play and more negatively when their daughters do, thus "confirming" that boys are more physical than girls. So do boys play with trucks and girls with dolls because *they* want to or because that's what their parents want them to? Think about that the next time you're looking for a gift for your baby.

Although mothers and fathers generally treat their sons and daughters in

*"I gotta go play with my doll now, so that I'll be a
really great Dad someday."*

the same sex-stereotyped ways—pushing girls to be more "feminine" and boys
to be more "masculine"—fathers have a greater tendency to do it. "Fathers
are likely to cuddle infant daughters gently but to engage in rough-and-tumble
activities with sons," writes Biller. In addition, Biller has found that "fathers
are more apt to accept a temperamentally difficult male infant but to withdraw
from a female infant who presents similar problems (see pages 89–96 for
more on temperament).

Biller warns, however, that fathers are not always discriminating when treating boys and girls differently. "The child's reaction can be a major factor; in
general, infant sons may actually display more positive emotional reactions
than daughters do when fathers engage them in physically stimulating play."

The whole point of this section is to get you to see how easy it is to fall into
sex-stereotype traps. Sure, you'll still probably treat girls a little differently
from boys; that's normal. But hopefully, now that you're a bit more aware of the
dynamics, you'll be able to avoid the larger problems and give your kids a
richer childhood experience.

If you have a boy, encourage him to communicate as much as he can. Don't
discourage him from crying or from playing with dolls, and teach him that
asking for help isn't a bad (unmanly) thing. If you have a daughter, encourage

"We're calling her Fred, after her father."

her to play physically and teach her that assertiveness and independence aren't unfeminine.

But whether you have a boy or a girl, make sure you aren't forcing your child into a type of behavior that doesn't fit his or her character or temperament. "Trying to force a boy or a girl into a straightjacket conception of appropriate sex-role behavior is certainly not in the child's best interests," writes Biller. "But neither is trying to pressure a child into behaving in a so-called nonsexist manner when he or she naturally appears comfortable with more traditional expectations." The bottom line is that some boys, if you give them a Barbie to play with, will tear her head off and use her legs as a double-barreled shotgun; and some girls are going to want to wear lace everywhere they go.

Planes, Trains, and Automobiles

What's Going On with the Baby

Physically

♦ Your baby is still conserving a lot of his physical energy in preparation for taking his first steps.

♦ He can nevertheless get himself to a standing position by straightening his legs and pushing off from his hands, and may even be able to stand up from a squatting position.

♦ He may be able to stand without any support and will try to do two activities at the same time, such as standing and waving. He may even try to squat down to pick up a toy.

♦ He can climb up stairs holding on to a railing and can walk holding on to only one of your hands.

♦ He adores rough play—wrestling, rolling around on the floor, being held upside down, and bouncing on your knees.

♦ He can turn the pages of a book, but not as accurately as he'd probably like to.

♦ He still can't release grasped objects exactly when and how he wants to.

Intellectually

♦ One day this month, your newly upright baby will be leaning against a chair and he'll accidentally make it move a little. He'll immediately understand that *he's* the one responsible and will do it again. And again. He may, in fact, spend the rest of the day (and the month, for that matter) pushing the chair around the house.

- Imitation reaches new heights this month. But rather than mimicking specific actions, he's now able to imitate *concepts*, or even a series of actions. He'll now hide things and get you to look for them, feed you, and try to brush his own teeth and get himself dressed.
- He'll spend a lot of time this month dropping small objects into larger containers, learning the difference between big and small, container and contained, "in" and "out."
- He's also expanding his knowledge about symbols. He's fascinated by books but doesn't really know what to make of them. He'll poke at the pictures in a book, intrigued by the idea that he can *see* an object but can't pick it up.
- Although still convinced that he's running the world, he's discovering that his body has certain limitations. If some precious object is out of reach, he'll push you toward it, trying to get you to reach it for him, thus using you as a tool.

Verbally

- Although his vocabulary is growing, he's nowhere near being able to put together sentences. But he'll babble in long "paragraphs" and toss in an occasional recognizable word.
- Interestingly, the sounds he uses in his babbling are specific to his native language, and he can no longer produce some of the ones he could even a few months ago.
- Whenever he learns a new word, he'll repeat it to himself dozens of times.
- He recognizes the symbolic use of words: he'll say "yum" if you're talking about ice cream, "meow" if you point out a cat.
- He's developed an incredible ability to hear what he wants to: he'll completely ignore a shouted "get away from that stove," but will stop whatever he's doing and rush to your side if you whisper "ice cream" from another zip code.

Emotionally/Socially

- Besides happy and sad, your baby is now capable of other, more sophisticated emotions. If you play with another baby, for example, he'll become jealous and protest loudly. He's also getting much more demonstrative, and will show genuine tenderness and affection to you as well as to his stuffed animals.
- He also understands approval and disapproval. When he cleans his plate, he'll joyously shout for you to come look, and he'll beam with pride at

having done something good. If he's done something he shouldn't have, though, he knows it and will bow his head sheepishly in anticipation of a few sharp words. Generally, he wants to please you, but he also needs to displease you to learn how you'll react.

♦ He may also be afraid of growing up and may regress emotionally as well as physically to a time when he was a baby and you took care of him.

♦ Strange as it sounds, your baby is already beginning to establish his or her own sexual identity. Girls begin to identify with their mother and other females and do what they do, while boys will identify with you and other men and want to do what you do.

What You're Going Through

Fear of Sexual Feelings

This may very well be the most controversial section in this book. So before you continue, you've got to promise that you'll keep an open mind and read all the way to the end.

Imagine this: you're rolling around on the floor with your baby, having the time of your life, or you're standing by your sleeping child's bed, stroking his beautiful, perfect cheek. Then, without warning, you get, well, aroused.

Now before you throw this book down and report me to the police, keep in mind that the overwhelming majority of mental health professionals say that it is *perfectly normal* for a parent to experience brief sexual feelings toward his or her child. "Most parents feel physical pleasure toward their babies," writes psychiatrist Stanley Greenspan. "For some, these pleasures are translated into fleeting sexual feelings."

Normal or not, feeling sexual desire—even briefly—for a child can be especially terrifying for men. You might be afraid that someone will accuse you of being a child molester, or that you actually are one and won't be able to control your unnatural "urges." Or that you might have to be locked up to protect your children. Or that you're completely insane.

Despite everything we hear about the "epidemic of sexual abuse," the truth is that well over 99 percent of parents never abuse anybody. So the odds are pretty slim that you'll do anything even remotely improper. Nevertheless, many men (and women as well) are so afraid and feel so guilty about their feelings that they withdraw from their children and stop playing with them, picking them up, or cuddling with them.

If you find yourself reacting in this way, stop it right now. "If you withdraw

"I did ask her and she said to ask you where I came from."

your physical displays of affection," says clinical psychologist Aaron Hass, "your child may believe there is something wrong with being affectionate in that manner. And if you stop hugging your child, you will miss the opportunity to enhance, in a very primal way, the bond between the two of you."

By reading this section you have, without even being aware of it, taken a very important step toward understanding and dealing with your momentary sexual feelings. Simply being aware of how normal these feelings are, says Dr. Greenspan, can "inhibit you from acting inappropriately" and "keep your special relationship with your baby from being dominated by fear."

Of course, if you're seriously worried that your feelings toward your child are inappropriate, and/or if you're having trouble managing them, get some professional help quickly. And don't worry, telling your therapist about your feelings will not get you arrested.

More Worries about the Baby's Health

For the first few months of your baby's life, you depended on your doctor to keep you informed as to how the baby was doing. And had there been any major problem (neurological defects, Down syndrome, and so on), or anything amiss with your baby's growth or development, you would have heard about it by now.

But most problems that affect children aren't easy to spot. And now that your baby is older and his well-baby checkups are farther apart, your pediatrician will rely more on you and your daily observations about your baby's behavior to make any diagnoses. Here are the kinds of things you should be looking out for:

♦ Is the baby having trouble manipulating objects or moving around? Delays in developing sensory/motor skills can cause delays in language development as well.

♦ Is the baby using her body fairly symmetrically? Does she use one hand (or foot, or eye) more than the other?

♦ Is the baby having trouble eating or swallowing food? Besides resulting in nutritional deficiencies and general health problems, these problems may interfere with your baby's using his jaw, lips, and tongue. Once again, language and cognitive skills can be seriously (negatively) affected.

♦ Has your baby lost previously attained skills? Did he used to babble and coo but suddenly stop? Does she no longer react when people come and go? This could be an indication of a hearing problem, which, again, can affect language development.

♦ Is the baby not achieving, within a month or two, the milestones described in the "What's Going On with the Baby" sections in this book?

♦ Does the baby seem uninterested in exploring his surroundings?

♦ Has your baby undergone a major change in temperament? (See pages 89–96.) But remember: difficult temperament by itself is *not* an indication of any kind of disability.

In most cases, the "problem" behaviors you identify will turn out to be perfectly normal. But that doesn't mean you should stop paying attention. Here are some things you can do to reassure yourself:

♦ Spend some time studying the "What's Going On with the Baby" sections of this book. The more you know about what your baby is and isn't capable of, the less you'll worry.

♦ Don't worry that your doctor—or your partner—will think you're asking too many questions or becoming overly concerned. You (or your insurance company) are paying your doctor more than enough for him or her to listen respectfully to any questions you might have.

♦ If, after talking to your doctor, you're still not satisfied (or you think you're being ignored), get another opinion.

♦ Keep a detailed log of things your child does (or doesn't do) that concern you, when they happen, and under what circumstances.

♦ Men have a tendency to ignore their own health concerns either because they hope whatever's worrying them will go away or because they're afraid the doctor will confirm their worst suspicions. If you want to ignore something that's been bothering you, that's your own prerogative. But don't apply the same standard to your baby. You may not be the most experienced parent in the world, but your gut reactions about what ails your children are usually pretty good and should be acted on. Of course, this doesn't mean bringing the baby into the emergency room every day, but an occasional call to your doctor's advice nurse is fine. If there is something to worry about, you're better off knowing sooner than later, when the problem will be much harder to deal with.

You and Your Baby

Planes, Trains, and Automobiles

When my older daughter was only six months old, my wife and I decided it was about time to take that honeymoon trip we'd been putting off since we'd gotten married. So we traded in a few years' worth of frequent-flier miles, and the three of us took off on a month-long trip to New York, France, Israel, and Phoenix. All in all, it was a great trip.

While your first trip with your baby is not likely to be as big an expedition as ours, sooner or later you're going to want to pack up the family and go somewhere.

What to Do Before You Go

♦ Spend some time planning your itinerary. You can take babies under about seven months just about anywhere anytime. After your baby has learned to walk, however, it's best to limit your destinations. Seven cities in four days is hard for even the most seasoned adult traveler.

♦ If possible, pick destinations that won't be terribly crowded; large groups of unfamiliar people may spook babies and toddlers alike.

♦ Get your tickets in advance. There's no sense standing in lines if you don't have to.

♦ Travel during off-peak times. Christmas Day, New Year's Day, and Thanksgiving Day (as opposed to the days before or after), for example, are good. If you're driving, there'll be less traffic on the road; if you're traveling some other way, you'll find a lot more empty seats, meaning more room to stretch out or run around.

♦ Red-eye flights may increase the chances your baby will sleep on the plane, and can also help get the jet-lag acclimation process under way.

♦ Prepare for jet-lag/time differences before you leave. You can keep the kid up late, put him to bed early, and so forth. Also adjust meal times.

♦ Prepare your child for the upcoming trip by talking about it regularly. Make it sound like it's going to be the most fun anyone has ever had.

♦ Schedule a doctor's appointment (for your child) for a few weeks before you leave. Tell your pediatrician where you're going and ask for the names of a few good local doctors. Also ask him or her to suggest any medical supplies you should bring along. If your child is taking any medication and will come anywhere near running out while you're on the road, get an extra prescription.

What to Bring

No matter where you go, the trick to making things run smoothly on a trip away from home is to surround your baby with as many familiar things as possible. This will help minimize the shock of the new routine and scenery. Whatever your destination, then, you'll probably need most of the following:

♦ Eating utensils and bibs.

♦ If you're traveling overseas and will be using powdered formula, plan on bringing some bottled water.

♦ Car seat. Doubles nicely as a high chair if you really need to restrain your baby while she's eating.

♦ A good backpack. It'll free up both your arms so you can schlep the six tons of other baby-related stuff you'll be needing.

♦ A portable crib. Or, if you'll be staying in a hotel, call ahead to reserve one.

♦ A first aid kit (see page 140 for the ingredients).

♦ A stroller that collapses compactly enough so you can take it on the plane.

♦ Lots of familiar toys, stuffed animals, favorite foods.

♦ Bring only what you're absolutely sure you'll need. If you aren't going trekking in the Himalayas, for example, there's really no sense taking along a large number of disposable diapers—they're available just about anywhere. The first thing my wife and I did when we arrived in New York was get a huge cardboard crate and ship home about half of the stuff we'd brought.

Once You Get There

♦ Keep up the routines you've established at home. Read, sing, play at the same times if you can. This is especially important for predictable babies (see page 91).

♦ Don't overbook activities. One or two excursions a day is plenty.

♦ Pick up local parenting publications (they're usually free) in whatever city or cities you're going to. You can order copies of these publications before you go by contacting Parenting Publications of America, 12715 Path Finder Lane, San Antonio, TX 78230-1532, (210) 492-3886, 492-3887 (fax); parpubs@aol.com.

♦ Keep a sharp eye on baby/relative contact. If friends and relatives haven't seen the baby for a while or are meeting him for the first time, they'll all want to hold, squeeze, cuddle, and entertain. This can freak out even the calmest of babies. Be especially sensitive if your baby is going through a period of stranger or separation anxiety.

♦ If you're planning to leave the baby with a sitter or a relative, have her or him come early so the two of them can get to know each other for a few minutes.

♦ Stay away from meats, fish, eggs, and dairy products. If you're going to get food poisoning on the road, it'll probably come from one of those food groups. And if you're traveling overseas, stay away from water, milk, juice, raw foods, and anything served by street vendors.

Traveling by Car

♦ For short trips, try to leave an hour or so before your baby's usual nap time and, once he falls asleep, drive as far as you can while his nap lasts.

♦ For longer trips, consider doing your driving from 4 P.M. to midnight. That way, you'll only have a few hours of entertainment and stops for feedings before baby goes to sleep for the night.

♦ If you need to drive during the day, you or your partner should ride in the back seat with the baby in hour or two-hour shifts to keep him amused and awake. Car travel tends to knock babies out and can really screw up their sleep schedules.

♦ Take lots of breaks and make sure everyone has plenty of opportunity to stretch, unwind, and relax. Stop at interesting places, pet the cows, watch the road-repair crews, point out new sights (forests, cloud shapes, and so forth), sing songs, read stories. Going through an automatic car wash can be a thrill for some kids, but for others it can be terrifying. Whatever you do, have fun.

♦ Put the car seat in the middle of the back seat; it's safest there.

♦ Lock car doors from the inside.

♦ Never, never leave your child alone in a car. Babies can suffocate a lot faster than you might think.

GOOD THINGS TO BRING IN THE CAR

- Lots of food and drink.
- Lots and lots of books.
- Stickers, markers, crayons, paper, and other art supplies.
- Magnetic puzzles.
- A battery-operated tape recorder (if you don't have one in the car) and a good selection of music. Make sure to bring some you like as well.

One warning: if you have to slam on your brakes at sixty miles an hour, every object you have in your car is a potential projectile. So before you bring anything into the car, think about whether you'd like to be hit in the head by it.

Traveling by Plane

- Get to the airport early. Let the baby run around and tire himself out. This may make the flight a little easier on everyone.
- Try to get bulkhead seats (usually the first row)—they generally offer a little more room, and you won't have to worry that your child will kick the seat of the people in front of you. Also, ask to be seated next to an empty seat if possible. Be sure to hold your absolutely adorable baby in your arms while you're asking—this can improve your chances of getting what you want.
- *Don't* board early. Instead, send your partner on with the carry-on stuff while you stay out in the lounge, letting the kids run themselves ragged until the last minute. Why spend any more time cooped up in the airplane than you absolutely have to?

The All-Purpose Travel Bag

If there's ever any danger of getting separated from your luggage (even if most of it is just in the trunk of your car), you should have a well-stocked bag with the necessary "emergency" supplies:

- Diapers and wipers.
- Toys (one for each hour of travel time); mirrors and suction-cup rattles are big hits with babies.
- Food.
- Something to suck on (pacifiers, teething rings, and so forth).
- A few books.
- Some favorite comfort items (blankets, teddy bears, and so on).

Either way, you should at least be aware of your insurance options. Basically, there are two types of life insurance on the market: term and cash value; each is further divided into several subcategories. Here's a brief overview:

TERM
There are three types of term insurance, and they all share these features:
- Fairly low cost, especially in the early years.
- Premiums increase over time as your odds of dying go up.
- Policies are in effect only for a specified period of time.
- No cash value accumulation.

Here are your basic term insurance choices:
- Renewable term. You can renew the policy annually. Death benefit generally remains level, while premiums increase over time.
- Level premium. The death benefit and the premium remain the same for a specified period of time, usually five, ten, or twenty years.
- Decreasing premium. The death benefit decreases each year, while premiums remain the same.

CASH VALUE
There are an increasing number of cash value insurance products available. Despite their differences, they all share the following features:
- These policies are essentially a combination of term insurance and a savings plan. A portion of your premium pays for pure term insurance. The balance is deposited into some kind of side fund on which you can earn interest or dividends.
- These policies tend to offer—initially—very competitive interest rates. The rate is usually guaranteed for a year, but then drops to whatever the market is paying.
- You can pay pretty much whatever you want to. But if your payment isn't enough to cover the insurance cost, the balance is taken out of your side fund, reducing your cash value.
- The cash benefit accumulates tax-free, and you can borrow against it or withdraw from it during your lifetime.
- If properly placed in trust, the entire cash and accumulated savings can go to your heirs free of income tax.

Here are your cash value choices:
- Whole life. Locks in a death benefit, cash values, and premium. The side fund is invested by the insurance company.

Picking a Financial Planner

Since most states don't have laws regulating or accrediting financial planners (who may also call themselves "advisors," "consultants," or "managers"), just about anyone can set up shop to dole out financial advice and sell products.

Most financial planners are paid on a commission basis, meaning that there's always at least the possibility of a conflict of interest. (In other words, whether or not your investments do well, the financial planner is assured his commission.) Commissions typically range from as low as 4 percent on some mutual funds to the entire first year's premium on a cash value life insurance policy. Others are paid on a fee basis and typically charge from $50 to $250 per hour.

This doesn't mean, of course, that fee-based planners are inherently better than their commission-based colleagues (although many experts believe that you'll be happier, and possibly richer, with someone who charges a fee). Your goal is to find someone you like and who you believe will have your best interests at heart. Here are a few things you can do to help you weed out the losers:

- ♦ Get references from friends, business associates, and so forth. Alternatively, the Institute of Certified Financial Planners (800) 282-7526 will give you some local references, and the National Association of Personal Financial Advisors (800) 366-2732 makes referrals only of fee-based (as opposed to commission-based) planners.
- ♦ Select at least three potential candidates and set up initial consultations (which shouldn't cost you anything). Then conduct tough interviews. Here's what you want to know:

- ♦ Universal life. Similar to Whole life, except that you can change the premium payment and death benefits anytime. And since the side fund is invested in fixed-income home securities (bonds and so forth), your cash values can fluctuate.
- ♦ Variable life. Similar to Universal, except that you have a bit more input into how your side fund is invested. Your choices usually include money markets, government securities, corporate bonds, growth, fixed-income, or total-return portfolios.

So how can you possibly make a choice between term and cash value?

◊ Educational background. Not to be snobby here, but the more formal the education—especially in financial management—the better. Watch out for fancy initials: many planners prominently display the letters CFP (for Certified Financial Planner) after their names. Forbes magazine recently called the CFP credential "meaningless."

◊ Level of experience. Unless you've got money to burn, let your niece break in her MBA on someone else. Stick to experienced professionals with at least three years in the business.

◊ Profile of the typical client. What you're looking for is a planner who has experience working with people whose income level and family situation are similar to yours.

◊ Compensation. If fee-based, how is the fee calculated? If commission, what are the percentages on each product offered? Any hesitation to show you a commission schedule is a red flag.

◊ Get a sample financial plan. You want to see what you're going to be getting for your money. Be careful, though: fancy graphics, incomprehensible boilerplate language, and expensive leather binders are often used to distract you from the report's lack of substance.

◊ References. How long have customers been with the planner? Are they happy? Better off? Any complaints or weaknesses?

♦ Check your prospective planner's record with state and federal regulators. You can call the federal Securities and Exchange Commission (202) 272-7450 or your state's equivalent to check on disciplinary action and to see whether your candidates have ever been sued.

Financial author and counselor Eric Tyson has some fairly strong views on the subject: "Cash value insurance is the most oversold insurance and financial product in the history of the industry," he writes. His solution?

Unless you have a high net worth, get yourself a term insurance policy with the following features:

♦ Guaranteed renewable (you don't want to be canceled if you get sick).

♦ Level premiums for five to ten years (that way you won't need to get a physical exam every year).

♦ A price you can live with. Costs for the very same policy can vary by as much as 200–300 percent, so shop around. (Since a rather big chunk of your premium is going to some agent in the form of commission, you can cut your costs way down by buying a "no load" or "low load" policy.)

WHEN YOU SHOULD BUY CASH VALUE INSURANCE

♦ Currently, an individual can leave up to $600,000, and a couple can leave up to $1,200,000 to beneficiaries *without* having to pay federal estate taxes. If you aren't worth this much, or don't expect to be when you die, stick with term.

♦ If you own a small business that's worth more than $1 million, cash value insurance makes sense, unless you have enough in liquid assets to pay off the estate taxes your heirs will owe.

Notes:

There Now, That Wasn't So Bad, Was It?

What's Going On with the Baby

Physically

♦ Still building toward walking, your baby can now get to a standing position from a squat and can lower herself gracefully from standing to sitting.

♦ She's also getting more confident about combining standing and walking. She can turn 90 degrees, stoop to pick things up, and walk holding on to you with one hand while clutching a favorite toy (or two or three) in the other. She might even experiment with taking a few backward steps.

♦ If your baby does take a few steps this month, she'll still use crawling as her main means of transportation.

♦ She can take simple covers off containers (but probably not screw-tops), and she'll help you dress and undress her (well, at least she *thinks* she's helping . . .).

♦ She's finally mastered her opposable thumb and can now pick up tiny objects between her thumb and pointing finger.

♦ She's also expressing a strong preference for "handedness," using one hand for grasping, the other for manipulating. If you put an object in her "passive" hand, she'll transfer it to the "active" one.

♦ She's now learned to store objects. If she's holding one thing in each hand and you offer her a third, she now wants to get control of all three; she'll transfer the contents of one hand to her mouth or armpit and *then* pick up the third object with the free hand.

Intellectually

♦ One of the most important intellectual accomplishments of your baby's first year is her ability to retain a visual image of an object she has seen before but that is currently out of sight.

♦ By the end of this month, your baby will be able to demonstrate this ability by searching—in more than one place—for objects she has seen but that she didn't see you hide.

♦ In another major intellectual leap this month, your baby will begin using trial and error to solve her problems and overcome obstacles.

♦ As annoying as it may get, it's important to recognize that your baby's constant banging, building and knocking over, and putting things in and dumping them out are important learning activities that are teaching her more about the multiple properties of the objects in her world. Adding water to sand changes the way the sand feels (and tastes); dropping marbles into a metal can produces a much different sound than dropping them into a plastic box; and dumping them onto the living room rug isn't nearly as much fun as watching them bounce and roll around after dumping them on the vinyl kitchen floor.

Verbally

♦ She probably has a vocabulary of six to eight real words, as well as five or six more sound words, such as *moo, woof,* or *boom.*

♦ Her passive vocabulary is significantly larger, and she'll gleefully identify quite a few of her body parts, as well as such familiar objects as you and your partner, her bottle, and her crib.

♦ She still doesn't know much about the symbolic use of words. If you point to a book at a friend's house and say, "Look at the book," your baby may be confused. In her world, the word *book* applies only to the ones at home.

Emotionally/Socially

♦ She actively tries to avoid doing things she knows you don't like, and loves your applause and approval.

♦ She's not always cooperative and will regularly test your limits (and your patience). She also is developing a basic sense of right and wrong and shows guilt when she does something wrong.

♦ She's developing a sense of humor and finds incongruities most entertaining. If you tell her a dog says "moo," or if you crawl or pretend to cry, she'll laugh hysterically.

♦ In her home, where she feels most secure, your baby will play with other

kids and may share some of her toys with them. In less secure environments, however, she's not nearly as sociable and will not stray far from you.
♦ She's got some pretty firm ideas of what she wants and will do what she can (cry, have a tantrum, smile sweetly) to influence your decisions.

What You're Going Through

Anger

While my wife was pregnant with our first child, I spent a lot of time thinking about the things I would never do once I became a father. First on my list was No Hitting the Kids. Then I thought about all those parents (including my own) I'd seen over the years scream at their children in the grocery store or

"If you ask me, this kid isn't lost. His parents just made a run for it."

the post office. "How weak," I remember thinking to myself. "If people can't control themselves any better than that, they really shouldn't be parents." I quickly and rather smugly added No Yelling at the Kids to my list.

One afternoon my daughter woke up from her nap crying like she never had before. I knew she wasn't tired, so I checked to see if her diaper was full (it wasn't), whether her clothes were binding her (they weren't), and even took her temperature (normal). She didn't respond to my comforting words or my requests to stop crying and tell me what was wrong (at six months, why should she?), and she continued howling. I was alone in the house, and after half an hour I'd had enough. I was frustrated and angry. So angry, in fact, that I felt like throwing my baby out the window and driving away.

Almost immediately, though, I was nearly overcome with feelings of embarrassment and disappointment for having let my emotions get away from me. I also felt like a complete failure as a father for having had such horrible thoughts about my own baby. It's no wonder that, in the words of psychologist Lawrence Kutner, "Anger—no, fury—is among the 'dirty little secrets' of parenthood."

"While parents talk about and glorify their feelings of love and protectiveness, their normal and often predictable moments of rage toward their children are seldom brought into the open," writes Kutner. "It is as if acknowledging the intensity of their anger is an admission of inadequacy or failure. If we deny it, perhaps it will go away, or we can convince ourselves that it never happened at all."

COPING WITH ANGER

"The conflicts that trigger the most intense responses often tell us more about ourselves than about our children," says Kutner. "Our most dramatic reactions to our children's behavior often come when we're feeling hurt. The child most likely to set off that strong, emotional response is the one who is most like us—especially when that child reminds us of things we don't particularly like about ourselves."

In addition, of course, things like job pressures, financial difficulties, health problems, or even car trouble can be redirected toward our kids and make us lash out at them. Whatever the reason for your anger, remember that there's nothing wrong with *feeling* it—even when it's directed at your kids. It's what you *do* with your anger, however, that can be a problem. Here are some suggestions that will help you understand, and better deal with, your anger.

- ♦ **Change your perspective.** Although your child may periodically do something deliberately to annoy you, many of his actions are really beyond his control. "A child's ability to bring out anger in his parents is usually

If You Lose Control . . .

Even parents with the best intentions accidentally lose control. If you do:

♦ Apologize. Explain to your child that you lost your temper. Make sure she knows that it was her *behavior* you didn't like, not her as a person, that you love her, and that you'll never hit her again.

♦ Don't go overboard, though. Resist the urge to punish yourself for your mistakes by being extra lenient with your child. You're only human, so lighten up.

Remember, anger can be just the first step in a vicious circle: something angers you enough that you lose control; feeling out of control makes you angrier; and feeling angry makes you feel even more out of control.

Unchecked, this process can escalate into physical and emotional abuse (which, besides screaming, can include insulting, humiliating, or withholding love). If you're worried that you might lose control again, get some help immediately: call a friend, a therapist, your child's pediatrician, or even a local parental-stress hotline (see also some of the suggestions for dealing with crying on pages 44–45). And if you're worried that your partner might prove to be violent, suggest she do the same.

a sign of normal development," says Kutner. "A toddler who is testing the limits of her independence will reject her parents occasionally, ignoring their pleas."

♦ **"Keep your sense of humor,"** says Ellen Galinsky. It may be a pain to clean up, but drawing on the walls with lipstick can be funny—if you let it.

♦ **Take regular breaks.** This can help keep minor annoyances from accumulating and boiling over. Make sure your partner gets plenty of time off too.

♦ **Give yourself a time-out.** Remove yourself from the situation and your child *before* you do something you'll regret for a long, long time.

♦ **Watch what you say.** Don't insult or humiliate your child. If you must criticize her, do it in private. Contrary to the old adage "Sticks and stones may break my bones, but names will never hurt me," calling your baby names can, in fact, have greater long-term negative impact than hitting.

◊ Use "I" messages: "*I* don't like it when you scratch me—it hurts," is a much more effective message than "*You're* a bad girl because you scratched me."

◊ Saying things like "You always . . ." or "You never . . ." can fill a child

with a sense of futility, a conviction that she'll fail no matter what she
does or how hard she tries.

◊ Avoid mixed messages. Yelling at your child to stop yelling will probably
not do you a lot of good.

♦ **Watch what you do.** "Children learn as much or more about the expression of anger from watching their parents when they are angry as they do
from verbal explanations or punishment," say Barbara and Philip Newman.
So don't let your toddler see you vent steam in a physical way; he won't be
able to understand your anger and might even be afraid that you'll turn on
him. He could also try to imitate you, and might hurt himself, someone
else, or someone's property.

♦ **Get physical.** Taking a long jog, punching a pillow, and taking a boxing
class are good ways to let off some steam. If there are any batting cages
nearby, try them out—if you squint, slow-moving softballs can look an
awful lot like a human head . . .

You and Your Baby

Discipline Update

When I was a kid, one of my father's favorite sayings was, "You're free to
swing your arms around any way you want. But that freedom ends right where
someone else's nose begins." In a nutshell, teaching your child this lesson—
to be respectful of other people's noses—is the primary goal of discipline.

A few months ago this was a concept your baby couldn't possibly have
grasped. And the only way for you to control his evil impulses was to distract
him with a toy and hope he'd forget about whatever it was he shouldn't have
been doing. But your baby's memory has been improving every day, and by the
time he's a year old one toy just won't do the trick anymore; now you'll need
two or three. And pretty soon, toys won't work at all.

When this happens, you'll face two major challenges, say the Newmans:
making a smooth transition from "nurturing protector to the force for law and
order," and combining "empathic caring" with "firm protectiveness."

The first step toward accomplishing these goals is to set reasonable, consistent limits. Here are a few things that will make this a lot easier:

♦ Limit potential risks. Basically, this means childproofing the hell out of
your house and keeping anything you really want to stay in one piece as far
away from the baby as possible. (To minimize problems elsewhere, ask
your parents and in-laws to take similar preventive measures.)

- Give the baby a safe place to explore.
- Have plenty of substitutes available: old phones and remote controls, spare computer keyboards, and so on. But be prepared: some kids can tell instinctively that what you're giving them isn't the real thing, and they won't be amused.
- Stop dangerous behavior immediately, but *subtly*. If your baby is pounding on a plate-glass window with his toy hammer and you scream, drop your coffee, and leap across the room to wrestle him to the ground, he'll find your reaction so much fun that he'll be sure to repeat exactly the behavior that provoked it the first time.
- Be tolerant of your baby's "negativity." Your baby's "no's" are an important part of his developing identity. Giving your baby some decision-making control will help him accept the limits you set.
- Spend some serious time trying to figure out what the baby needs. Researcher Donelda Stayton and her associates found that early obedience (in nine-to-

twelve-month-olds) was related to the sensitivity of responsiveness to infant signals, *not* to the frequency of commands or forcible interventions.

While setting limits is important, it's really only half the battle. "If children are to correct their own behavior," write the Newmans, "they must know what acts are considered appropriate as well as how to inhibit their inappropriate acts." And the way your child will learn these lessons is by watching you. "Parental modeling and reinforcement of acceptable behavior are significant in the development of internal control," write the Newmans.

Biting and Hitting

For some strange reason, right around their first birthdays, almost all babies go through a phase when they bite and/or hit people—strangers and loved ones alike. If (when) your baby starts, the first thing you need to do is find out why. Your baby may be biting or hitting because she's:

 ◆ Trying to express affection (you probably nibble gently on her and she may simply be trying to imitate you).
 ◆ Frustrated that she can't express herself verbally.
 ◆ Teething and trying to relieve her discomfort.
 ◆ Simply conducting an experiment to see how others will react.
 ◆ Tired, overstimulated, or frustrated.
 ◆ Trying to defend herself or her property.
 ◆ Imitating an older friend or sibling.

Fortunately, the hitting-and-biting phase usually lasts no longer than a few months (although, when you're getting bitten a few times a day, that can seem like a very long time). Here, however, are a few dos and don'ts that may make this painful period a little shorter:

 ◆ Don't get angry; it will only make her defensive.
 ◆ Don't slap or spank.
 ◆ Don't bite back or have the baby bite herself "to show her what it feels like"; this sets a rotten example and will only reinforce the behavior by implying that it's really okay.
 ◆ Do remove the baby promptly. If she's sitting on your lap and bites you, put her down for a minute (no longer); if she's hit or bitten someone else, take her away from that person for a minute.
 ◆ Don't say, "You're bad" or any variation on that theme. Instead say, "*Biting* is bad."
 ◆ Don't insist on an apology. There's almost no chance that your baby has

Keep Your Mouth Running

There's plenty of evidence that talking to your baby can have some very positive long-term effects. So as you go through the day, identify everything you can, tell the baby what you're doing, where you're going, what's going on outside, what the weather's like, who won last night's baseball games, and so on.

According to pediatrician Burton White, parents who raised babies who turned out to be gifted or at least bright did the following things to build their children's language skills from infancy:

◆ They identified the things their children were interested in and talked about them a lot.

◆ They engaged in fifteen to twenty verbal interchanges each hour, most lasting between twenty and thirty seconds.

◆ They rarely "taught" or lectured children. Instead, they spoke casually and conversationally.

◆ They spoke in full sentences, using words slightly above the child's apparent level of comprehension.

◆ They read picture books and stories from infancy, even though most of the kids didn't seem to be paying much attention until they were two.

any idea what regret is or that biting really hurts (babies this age are completely incapable of imagining anything from any other perspective than their own).

◆ Don't overreact. The baby might find your reaction so amusing that she'll bite or hit again just to get your attention.

◆ Do spend some time trying to figure out why your baby is biting or hitting. Is it happening at certain times of the day (right before nap time, for example)? Does she do it only to certain people?

◆ Do rethink your discipline policies. You may be setting so many limits that your baby may be trying to bite her way to freedom.

Weaning Your Baby from Breast or Bottle

Most pediatricians today agree that new mothers should breastfeed their babies for as long as possible—generally between six months and a year. What to do after that, however, is the source of far less agreement.

So should you stop breastfeeding completely now or gradually phase it out? Should you transition your baby from breast to bottle, or skip the bottle and go directly to cups? And if you've been bottle-feeding from the start, when should you stop? The answers, of course, are up to you, your partner, and your baby.

We're assuming here that your baby is eating at least *some* solid foods in addition to her breast- or bottle-feeding. Eventually, she'll get all her food via cup and utensils, but the process of weaning her completely can take months or even years. (My wife nursed our older daughter for nine months and our younger for two years.)

Why to Wean the Baby from the Breast (or at Least Cut Back Some)

♦ By one year, the baby's gotten most of the long-term health benefits from breastfeeding. At this point, breastmilk alone can't satisfy all the baby's needs and may, in fact, suppress her appetite for solids.

♦ Babies who fall asleep with a breast in their mouth (and many do), often leave their teeth soaking in a pool of milk—this can lead to tooth decay.

♦ Most babies nurse in some kind of reclining position. This allows fluid from the mouth back up into the Eustachian tubes and can cause ear infections.

♦ The baby may start (or may already be) using the breast as a comfort or sleep aid, thus delaying development of the ability to comfort herself or fall asleep by herself.

♦ You may be feeling that enough is enough: your partner's breasts have been at least partially off-limits for a year, and it's time to unlatch that baby. You may see your wife's refusal to do so as a kind of slap in your face.

Why to Wean the Baby from the Bottle (or Start Cutting Back)

♦ Babies tend to let formula or juice slosh around in their mouths for a while. Little teeth that soak up too much can rot.

♦ Your baby may fill herself up on liquids so much that she will lose interest in all those solid foods she needs for a well-balanced diet.

♦ By about fifteen months your baby may begin forming an emotional attachment to her bottle (just as she might to a blanket, thumb, or favorite stuffed animal). Emotional attachments are nice, but breaking an attachment to a bottle will be a lot easier now than in a few months, when the baby starts getting stubborn and contrary.

♦ Some experts believe that overdependence on the bottle can interfere with physical and mental developmental milestones and advise giving it up entirely by eighteen months.

Introduction to Potty Training

Have you heard the one about the kid who was toilet-trained at eight months? If you haven't, you soon will. But prepare yourself: it isn't a joke—or, at least, it isn't *supposed* to be one. People will tell you all sorts of things about the babies they knew who were out of diapers before they could walk. But no matter what anyone says, or how much you might want to believe the stories, they just aren't true.

First of all, there's no such thing as potty training; your child will learn to use the toilet on her own only when she's ready. And at eight months or even a year, she's simply incapable of controlling her bowels or bladder. Sure, she may grunt and groan while producing a bowel movement, and everyone in the house (except her, of course) will be able to smell it, but she has no idea there's any connection between the feeling she gets when she's filling a diaper and the actual contents. If anybody's being "trained" at this age it's the parents, who may have learned to recognize their baby's signals and rush her to the toilet. But rest assured, the baby can't do it on her own.

At about fifteen months your baby will begin associating what's in her diaper with herself and may announce from time to time that she's produced something. But only after the fact. At eighteen months she may occasionally announce that she is *about* to do something, but she still hasn't learned how to hold it in long enough to get to a toilet. For the best results, unless your child is extremely interested, wait until she's at least two before seriously starting to toilet "train" her.

In the meantime, however, you can help increase your child's awareness of what's going on in her diapers by talking about the process as it's happening. As you're changing her, show the baby what she's done, but don't emphasize the yuckiness of it. Instead, say something admiring, like "Hey, that's a pretty impressive load—someday you'll do this in the toilet like me and mommy."

♦ A hint for easing the process of giving up the bottle: If the baby protests her missing bottle, offer her some solid food first. The theory here is that if she's full before starting the bottle, she won't be as interested in it and will miss it less when it's gone.

Perfectly Good Reasons to Continue Limited Breastfeeding

♦ The baby likes it.
♦ Your partner likes it, likes the contact and connection with the baby, and doesn't want to give it up.
♦ It's more natural, cheaper, and more convenient than prepared food.

Making the Switch

On one occasion while my wife was still nursing, she got held up in meetings and couldn't get home to feed the baby. If our daughter had been used to taking a bottle, this wouldn't have been a problem. But I'd only tried once or twice to get her to take a bottle and hadn't put up much of a fight when she'd spit it out. My punishment for having been so lax was that I had to drive

---

Temperament Tidbits

How well your baby makes the transition from breastfeeding to bottle-feeding or cups may depend more on his temperament than on any other factor. According to temperament researcher Jim Cameron:

♦ Extremely active toddlers with high-frustration tolerance (they aren't easily frustrated) usually wean themselves. They prefer bottles to breast because of the convenience.
♦ Highly active, slow-to-adapt kids also like the independence and convenience of a bottle or cup during the day. But they'll still want to nurse in the morning and at night.
♦ Active kids who don't tolerate frustration as well, however, know that parents are quite helpful in overcoming frustration. To them, giving up nursing means giving up support and help from parents and they won't be in any hurry to do it.
♦ Slow-adapting kids see the breast as security and won't want to give it up without a fight, especially at night. A gradual phase-out is particularly important for these kids.
♦ Moderately high-energy, high-adjustability kids wean themselves naturally.
♦ Kids who are moderately high in activity level and moderately low in frustration tolerance are fairly ambivalent about weaning. They'll generally take their direction from you and your partner.

---

twenty miles to my wife's office—with the baby screaming at the top of her lungs—so she could nurse. The moral of the story is: start getting the baby used to taking a bottle as early as possible (but not before she's completely comfortable with the breast). Here are some things you can do to get even the most committed breastfeeder to give the bottle a try:

♦ Use smaller bottles and nipples. Keep experimenting until you find a size and style the baby likes. If she's got a pacifier, try a bottle nipple that is shaped like the one on her pacifier.

♦ When introducing the bottle, hold the baby in the position she's in for breastfeeding.

♦ Ease the transition by filling bottles or cups with expressed breast milk. Some women find pumping very painful, so leave this one up to your partner.

♦ Go slow. Introduce the bottle for a few minutes at first, then add a minute or two every day.

♦ Phase out gradually. Kids tend to be more attached to the morning and evening feedings, so start by eliminating your baby's midday feeding(s) first. If that goes well for a few days, drop the morning feeding next. Of course, exceptions can be made: we dropped the evening feeding first because our daughters were getting up at five in the morning to eat anyway. So why not nurse (and hope the baby goes back to sleep again), rather than get out of a warm bed.

♦ A tip: Make sure your partner is out of the house (or at least out of sight in another room) when you're trying to give the baby a bottle. If your partner (actually, her breasts) are within smelling distance, your baby may refuse the bottle.

♦ A warning: The American Academy of Pediatrics suggests not starting your baby on cow's milk until after the baby's first birthday.

When *Not* to Wean Your Baby

No matter how old your baby is or how long he's been breast- or bottle-feeding, there are a few really rotten times to try to wean him:

♦ Any impending or recent major transition that might make the baby feel vulnerable, out of control, and in need of extra parental support. Moving to a new home, the birth of a younger sibling or the announcement of pregnancy, a new baby-sitter, and starting day care are good examples.

♦ If the baby has been sick.

♦ If you or your partner are under some kind of extreme pressure.

♦ If the baby is teething.

Family Matters

Ch-Ch-Ch-Changing Relationships

Considering how small and helpless babies are, it's sometimes surprising just how much of an impact they can have on the lives of the adults around them. Just think, for example, about how different things are for you now compared to your prefatherhood life.

Babies create new relationships in people's lives simply by being born: you and your partner have gone from being children to being parents, your parents are now grandparents, your brothers and sisters are uncles and aunts, and so on. And naturally, those relationships (as well as the rights and responsibilities that go with them) will take some getting used to.

But perhaps babies' greatest power is their ability to change profoundly the relationships that had existed long before they were born.

Your Changing Relationship with Your Partner

"Most couples approach parenthood imagining the new baby will bring them closer together, giving them a new and deeper sense of 'us,'" writes researcher Jay Belsky. For most families, things ultimately work out this way. But Belsky found that in the early stages of parenthood a new baby "tends to push his mother and father apart by revealing the hidden and half-hidden differences in their relationship."

Not surprisingly, says Phil Cowan, "differences between partners lead to feeling distant, that feeling distant tends to stimulate conflict, and that increased conflict, in turn, affects both partners' feelings about the marriage."

Some of the differences are aggravated because, although their feelings about their relationship with each other are very similar, men and women rarely feel the same thing at the same time. Many women, for example, tend to experience a major drop in their level of satisfaction with the marriage within six months of the baby's birth. Among the common reasons for this are a woman's feelings about her postbirth body, her perception that her partner is less interested in her, and her dissatisfaction with the workload around the house.

Many men, too, go through a decline in satisfaction with their marriages, but usually not until twelve to eighteen months after the baby's birth. This is when financial issues, fears about not being loved by the baby, and feelings of being left out by their partners are uppermost in their minds.

Although declining satisfaction with a marriage sounds bad, Phil Cowan believes it doesn't necessarily have to be so. "Given that men's and women's

Baby's First Birthday Party

Let's get one thing straight: your baby's first birthday party is really more for you than for her. She won't help you put together the guest list, is too little to play Pin the Tail on the Donkey or to bob for apples, and will probably be more interested in the wrapping paper than in what's inside it.

Here are a couple of first birthday dos and don'ts:

♦ Don't knock yourself out planning special activities. At this age your baby will prefer the familiar to the new almost every time.

♦ Don't invite too many kids—two or three is plenty. And limit the adults to six or seven. Any more and you run the risk of overwhelming the baby.

♦ Don't make a huge cake (unless the adults plan to eat it). And remember: no nuts, honey, or cow's milk.

♦ Save the clowns and masks for next year or the year after. Kids under two or three are more often scared by masks than entertained.

♦ Keep the party short (no more than an hour) and try not to have it conflict with nap or sleep times or any other time when your baby tends to be cranky.

♦ Don't go overboard on gifts. And don't demand or even expect wild declarations of thanks or any other great performances for the cameras. It's just not going to happen.

♦ Give identical party favors to any other child guests. Make sure your baby gets one as well.

♦ Get presents (smaller ones) for any older or younger siblings.

♦ Keep a list (or have someone else do it) of who gave what so you can send thank-yous later.

energies are not infinitely expandable," he writes, "it may be adaptive for some energy to be diverted from the couple relationship in the service of attending to the needs of the infant or young child. . . . Those who can adopt the perspective that placing the marriage on the back burner is a regrettable but temporary state of affairs may be able to return to enhanced relationship satisfaction and quality in the future."

Here are a few of the very positive ways the baby can affect your life and your relationship with your partner.

♦ You may feel a sense of gratefulness to the baby for enabling you to feel what it's like to be loved and to love more deeply than you ever have before.

♦ For some men having a baby is like having a great new toy and may give you a chance to relive certain parts of your childhood.

♦ The baby may bring you and your partner closer together and may make the two of you feel more deeply committed to the marriage and to making it work. You now also have someone to pass along new and old family traditions to.

♦ The baby may give you and your partner a sense of tremendous pride at having jointly created something absolutely amazing.

Parent/Grandparent Relationships

THE GOOD . . .

♦ After becoming parents, most men feel closer to their parents, especially their fathers. Even those who don't feel closer are usually at least willing to end, or put behind them, long-running family disputes.

♦ Seeing your parents in action with your child may bring back happy memories of your own childhood. You may also be pleasantly surprised at how

"Do you remember any of those things people said we'd tell our grandkids someday?"

your parents have changed since you were young. The father who may not have had much time for you, for example, may now spend hours with his grandchild. And the mother who limited your junk food intake to half a stick of sugarless gum a week may be a little more relaxed now.

♦ Now that you know exactly how much work it is to be a parent, you may be feeling a bit more appreciative of what your own parents did—and sacrificed—for you.

♦ After all these years of being a child, you're in charge now; if they want to be with the baby, they'll have to do things *your* way.

♦ You'll develop a closer relationship with your in-laws.

THE BAD . . .

♦ Seeing your parents in action with your child may bring back unhappy memories of your own childhood. And if your parents are treating the baby differently than they treated you, you may be jealous, feeling that the love your baby is getting should really be yours.

♦ Your parents may not be supportive or accepting of your increased role in your child's life.

♦ They may want to assume a role in your child's life—either too involved or not involved enough—that you aren't happy with. Grandparents are free to love their grandchildren without any of the restrictions of parenthood, says psychologist Brad Sachs.

♦ There may be some friction between your parenting style and that of your parents, between the way you react to the baby's needs and the way they do. It's not uncommon to hear from one's parents statements such as: "I did a pretty good job of raising my own kids, so don't tell me how to . . ." or "Don't you think it's time she [your partner] stopped nursing that child?"

♦ If you think they did a lousy job as parents, you may be afraid of repeating their mistakes.

♦ If your parents live nearby, they may always be "in the neighborhood," and you might be seeing them more than you really care to.

♦ There may be disputes and power struggles between your parents and your partner's about their grandparental roles.

However your relationship with your parents and/or in-laws changes, remember this: "A loving and vigorous bond between the grandparent and grandchild," writes Sachs, "is not just related to, but *essential* to, the emotional health and stability of *all three generations.*"

Other Relationships

Without really thinking about it, you and your partner will find that your relationships with friends and other nonimmediate family members have changed.

♦ You may be interested (or at least more interested than you were before becoming a parent) in getting together with relatives your own age, especially those with kids, so that the next generation can get to know their cousins.

♦ Your circle of closer friends will gradually change to include more couples, especially couples with kids.

♦ While your child is young, she'll be happy to play with whomever you introduce her to, and her first friends are most likely going to be *your* friends' kids. But as she gets older and starts meeting other kids on her own in parks and preschools, your child will take on a more active role in the family social committee, and all of a sudden you'll find yourself socializing with *her* friends' parents.

♦ Relationships between you and other adults may continue longer than they otherwise might because the kids like getting together.

♦ Relationships can be affected by competition: whose kid walks, talks, reads, or even sings first. As minor as it sounds, this can have a dramatic effect on your friendships. My wife and I used to get together fairly regularly with a couple whose two kids were just a few months older than ours. We all had a lot in common and got along fine, but the woman couldn't stop comparing her kids to ours—usually right in front of them—and hers, surprisingly, always came up on the short end. It was all very nice to hear how great our kids were, but after a while my wife and I couldn't stand it any more and the friendship eventually fizzled out.

Going Public with Fatherhood

In the concluding chapter of *The Expectant Father* I painted a rather gloomy portrait of the ways men and women—both individually and collectively as a society—actively discourage men from getting involved with their children. Sadly, in the several years since the publication of that book, little has changed. Men still don't get the support and encouragement they so sorely need to assume a greater nurturing role.

Fortunately, though, more and more men are expressing their dissatisfaction with this Neanderthal status quo. And we're just now starting to see the results of a modest revolution that's been going on quietly for more than twenty years.

Today, some 90 percent of fathers (even those who don't or won't live with their kids) are present at their children's births—more than triple the percentage in 1974. Seventy-five percent of men say their jobs conflict with their family responsibilities—up from only 12 percent in 1977; 74 percent say they'd give up their fast-track job for a "daddy-track" job that would allow them to spend more time with their families; and 30 percent reported actually having turned down a job promotion or transfer for the same reason.

Of course, some of these dramatic changes may have been born out of economic necessity: more and more mothers are entering the workplace and someone else has to step in to share the child-care burden. But in my view, the more significant reason for the nurturing-father revolution has to do with men themselves.

Most men, especially those whose fathers were physically or emotionally absent, instinctively know what they missed when they were young. And just as they know they were deprived of a relationship with their fathers, they know that their fathers were deprived of relationships with them.

More than turning down a job promotion or transfer, the real measure of a man's commitment to a new kind of relationship with his kids is how he feels about being a father and about the impact fatherhood is having on his life.

In one major study, researchers found that fathers generally see fathering as an important and satisfying experience. They disagree that only mothers should be responsible for discipline or for caring for a sick child; rather, they consider parenting a partnership experience to be shared equally with their wives.

Clearly, things are changing for fathers—perhaps not as quickly as we would like, but they are changing. "Discussion is growing on on-line computer networks. Men's centers and private-practice therapists are beginning to offer fathers' groups," writes Steven Harris, editor of *Full-Time Dad* magazine. "Fathers are tentatively pushing their way into play-groups and other informal gatherings, once the domain of mothers exclusively. The life of the father is expanding, slowly but surely."

Still, far too many men continue to devalue the importance of the role they play in their children's lives. Too many children have missed having a relationship with their fathers, and too many fathers have missed having relationships with their children.

As a new father, you are in a unique position to break this cycle and to make the word *fatherhood* as synonymous with childrearing and nurturing as *motherhood*. And there's no better time to start than right now.

For most new fathers, the last few months of their first year as parents are a time of relative calm. They've dealt with the big emotional, professional, and personal hurdles of fatherhood and are now comfortably juggling their

"My father wakes up the sun every morning.
What does your father do?"

roles as husband, father, provider, and son. In short, they're finally feeling "like a family," and are entering what Bruce Linton calls the "community phase" of fatherhood.

As a result, says Linton, at this stage many new fathers feel ready to socialize—along with their partners and children—with other families, and use their fatherhood as a way to participate more actively in the public domain. They typically take on a more active role in their churches or synagogues, and they experience a heightened sense of *public* responsibility. Issues such as the quality of schools, city planning and zoning, the environment, and public safety become much more pressing than before.

Other researchers have confirmed Linton's theory. "Parenting brings new levels of insight and social commitment," write Barbara and Philip Newman, "that contribute in positive ways to the overall evolution of the culture."

In the introduction to this book, I quoted author Michael Levine, who said that "having children makes you no more a parent than having a piano makes you a pianist." Well, at this point you may not be any closer to being a pianist than you were a year ago. But there's no doubt that you're a parent. And a pretty good one at that.

Selected Bibliography

Books

Ames, Louise Bates, and Carol Chase Haber. *Your One Year Old: The Fun-Loving, Fussy 12- to 24-Month-Old.* New York: Delta, 1982.

Barry, Dave. *Bad Habits.* New York: Henry Holt, 1985.

Belsky, Jay, and John Kelly. *The Transition to Parenthood: How a First Child Changes a Marriage: Why Some Couples Grow Closer and Others Apart.* New York: Delacorte, 1994.

Berman, Phyllis W., and Frank A. Pedersen. *Men's Transitions to Parenthood: Longitudinal Studies of Early Family Experience.* Hillsdale, N.J.: Erlbaum, 1987.

Bettelheim, Bruno. *A Good Enough Parent: A Book on Child-Rearing.* New York: Vintage, 1987.

Biller, Henry B. *Fathers and Families: Paternal Factors in Child Development.* Westport, Conn.: Auburn House, 1993.

Biller, Henry B., and Robert J. Trotter. *The Father Factor: What You Need to Know to Make a Difference.* New York: Pocket Books, 1994.

Bluestine, Eric. *The Ways Children Learn Music: An Introduction and Practical Guide to Music Learning Theory.* Chicago: GIA Publications, 1995.

Bornstein, M. H., ed. *Handbook of Parenting.* Hillsdale, N.J.: Erlbaum, 1995.

Brazelton, T. Berry, and Bertrand Cramer. *The Earliest Relationship: Parents, Infants, and the Drama of Early Attachment.* Reading, Mass.: Addison-Wesley, 1990.

Bronstein, Phyllis, and Carolyn Pape Cowan, eds. *Fatherhood Today: Men's Changing Role in the Family.* New York: John Wiley & Sons, 1988.

Britton, James. *Language and Learning: The Importance of Speech in Children's Development.* New York: Penguin, 1970.

Brott, Armin, and Jennifer Ash. *The Expectant Father: Facts, Tips, and Advice for Dads-to-Be.* New York: Abbeville Press, 1995.

Butler, Dorothy. *Babies Need Books.* New York: Atheneum, 1980.

Canfield, Ken. *The Heart of a Father.* Chicago: Northfield, 1996.

Caplan, Frank, ed. *The First Twelve Months of Life.* New York: Grosset & Dunlap, 1973.

Cath, Stanley H., et al., eds. *Fathers and Their Families.* Hillsdale, N.J.: Analytic Press, 1989.

————. *Father and Child: Developmental and Clinical Perspectives.* Hillsdale, N.J.: Analytic Press, 1994.

Cowan, Carolyn Pape, and Philip A. Cowan. *When Partners Become Parents: The Big Life Change for Couples.* New York: HarperCollins, 1992.

Cullinan, Bernice E., and Lee Galda. *Literature and the Child,* 3d ed. Orlando, Fla.: Harcourt Brace, 1994.

Cutchins, Judy, and Ginny Johnston. *Parenting Papas: Unusual Animal Fathers.* New York: Morrow Junior Books, 1994.

Drobeck, Bruce. "The Impact on Men of the Transition to Fatherhood: A Phenomenological Investigation." Dissertation, 1990.

Eisenberg, Arlene, et al. *What to Expect the First Year.* New York: Workman, 1989.

Flint Public Library. *Ring a Ring O'Roses: Finger Plays for Pre-School Children.* Flint, Mich.: Flint Public Library, n.d.

Fraiberg, Selma H. *The Magic Years: Understanding and Handling the Problems of Early Childhood.* New York: Scribner's, 1959.

Galinsky, Ellen. *Between Generations: The Six Stages of Parenthood.* New York: Times Books, 1981.

Gordon, Edwin E. *A Music Learning Theory for Newborn and Young Children.* Chicago: GIA Publications, 1990.

Greene, Ellin. *Books, Babies, and Libraries: Serving Infants, Toddlers, Their Parents, and Caregivers.* Chicago: ALA Books, 1991.

Greenspan, Stanley, and Nancy Thorndike Greenspan. *First Feelings: Milestones in the Emotional Development of Your Baby and Child.* New York: Penguin, 1985.

Hanson, Shirley M. H., and Frederick W. Bozett. *Dimensions of Fatherhood.* Beverly Hills, Calif.: Sage, 1985.

Hass, Aaron. *The Gift of Fatherhood: How Men's Lives Are Transformed by Their Children.* New York: Fireside, 1994.

Hochschild, Arlie. *The Second Shift: Working Parents and the Revolution at Home.* New York: Viking, 1989.

Jacob, S. H. *Your Baby's Mind*. Holbrook, Mass.: Bob Adams, 1991.

Jordan, Pamela L. "The Mother's Role in Promoting Fathering Behavior." In *Becoming a Father: Contemporary Social, Developmental, and Clinical Perspectives*, J. L. Shapiro, et al., eds. New York: Springer Publications, 1995, pp. 61–71.

Karen, Robert. *Becoming Attached: Unfolding the Mystery of the Infant-Mother Bond and Impact on Later Life*. New York: Warner Books, 1994.

Kitzinger, S. *The Experience of Breastfeeding*. Middlesex, England: Penguin, 1987.

Kropp, Paul. *Raising a Reader: Make Your Child a Reader for Life*. New York: Doubleday, 1996.

Kutner, Lawrence. *Your School-Age Child*. New York: William Morrow, 1996.

Lamb, Michael E., ed. *The Role of the Father in Child Development*. New York: John Wiley, 1981.

Leach, Penelope. *Babyhood*. New York: Knopf, 1974 (1983).

Lehane, Stephen. *Help Your Baby Learn: 100 Piaget-Based Activities for the First Two Years of Life*. New York: Prentice Hall, 1976.

Linton, Bruce. "The Phases of Paternal Development: Pregnancy Through Twelve Months Post-Partum." Dissertation, 1991.

Marino, Jane, and Dorothy F. Houlihan. *Mother Goose Time: Library Programs for Babies and Their Caregivers*. New York: H. W. Wilson, 1992.

Marzollo, Jean. *Fathers and Babies*. New York: HarperPerennial, 1993.

Minnesota Fathering Alliance. *Working with Fathers: Methods and Perspectives*. Stillwater, Minn.: nu ink unlimited, 1992.

Newman, Barbara M., and Philip R. Newman. *Development Through Life: A Psychosocial Approach*, 6th ed. Pacific Grove, Calif.: Brooks/Cole Publishing, 1994.

Pagnoni, Mario. *Computers and Small Fries: A Computer-Readiness Guide for Parents of Tots, Toddlers and Other Minors*. Wayne, N.J.: Avery Publishing, 1987.

Parke, Ross D. *Fathers*, rev. ed. Cambridge, Mass.: Harvard University Press, 1996.

———. "Fathers and Families." In *Handbook of Parenting*, M. H. Bornstein, ed. Hillsdale, N.J.: Erlbaum, 1995.

Parke, Ross D., and Barbara R. Tinsley. "The Father's Role in Infancy: Determinants of Involvement in Caregiving and Play." In *The Role of the Father in Child Development*, Michael Lamb, ed. New York: Wiley, 1981.

Platt, Harvey J. *Your Living Trust and Estate Plan: How to Maximize Your Family's Assets and Protect Your Loved Ones*. New York: Allworth Press, 1995.

Pleck, Joseph H. "Are 'Family Supportive' Employer Policies Relevant to Men?" In *Men, Work, and Family,* Jane C. Hood, ed. Newbury Park, Calif.: Sage, 1993.

Pruett, Kyle D. "The Nurturing Male: A Longitudinal Study of Primary Nurturing Fathers." In *Fathers and Their Families,* Stanley Cath et al., eds. Hillsdale, N.J.: Analytic Press, 1989.

Sachs, Brad E. *Things Just Haven't Been the Same: Making the Transition from Marriage to Parenthood.* New York: William Morrow, 1992.

Schaffer, Judith, and Christina Lindstrom. *How to Raise an Adopted Child.* New York: Crown, 1989.

Sears, William, and Martha Sears. *The Baby Book: Everything You Need to Know about Your Baby—From Birth to Age Two.* New York: Little Brown, 1993.

Snarey, John. *How Fathers Care for the Next Generation: A Four-Decade Study.* Cambridge, Mass.: Harvard University Press, 1993.

Spangler, Doug. *Fatherhood: An Owner's Manual.* Richmond, Calif.: Fabus, 1994.

Spock, Benjamin, and Michael B. Rothenberg. *Dr. Spock's Baby and Child Care.* New York: Pocket Books, 1992.

Steinberg, David. *Fatherjournal.* Albion, Calif.: Times Change Press, 1977.

Sullivan, S. Adams. *The Father's Almanac,* rev. ed. New York: Doubleday, 1992.

Trelease, Jim. *The New Read-Aloud Handbook.* New York: Penguin, 1989.

Tyson, Eric. *Personal Finance for Dummies.* Foster City, Calif.: IDG Books, 1995.

Ulene, Art, and Steven Shelov. *Discovery Play: Loving and Learning with Your Baby.* Berkeley, Calif.: Ulysses Press, 1994.

White, Burton L. *The First Three Years of Life: The Revised Edition.* New York: Prentice Hall, 1985.

Journal Articles

Bailey, William T. "Fathers' Involvement and Responding to Infants: 'More' May Not be 'Better.'" *Psychological Reports* 74 (1994): 92–94.

———. "Psychological Development in Men: Generativity and Involvement with Young Children." *Psychological Reports* 71 (1992): 929–30.

Barrett-Goldfarb, Minna, and Grover J. Whitehurst. "Infant Vocalizations as a Function of Parental Voice Selection." *Developmental Psychology* 8, no. 2 (1973): 273–76.

Baumrind, Diana. "Current Patterns of Parental Authority." *Developmental Psychology Monograph* 4, no. 1, part 1 (1971): 1–101.

Cohn, Deborah A., et al. "Working Models of Childhood Attachment and Couple Relationships." *Journal of Family Issues* 13, no. 4 (1992): 432–49.

Condry, John, and Sandra Condry. "Sex Differences: A Study of the Eye of the Beholder." *Child Development* 47 (1976): 812–19.

Condry, John, and David F. Ross. "Sex and Aggression: The Influence of Gender Label on the Perception of Aggression in Children." *Child Development* 56 (1985): 225–33.

DeLuccie, Mary F. "Mothers as Gatekeepers: A Model of Maternal Mediators of Father Involvement." *Journal of Genetic Psychology* 156, no. 1 (1994): 115–31.

Deutsch, Francine M., et al. "Taking Credit: Couples' Reports of Contributions to Child Care." *Journal of Family Issues* 14, no. 3 (1993): 421–37.

Dickstein, Susan, and Ross D. Parke. "Social Referencing in Infancy: A Glance at Fathers and Marriage." *Child Development* 59 (1988): 506–11.

Fagot, Beverly I. "The Influence of Sex of Child on Parental Reactions to Toddler Children." *Child Development* 49 (1978): 459–65.

———. "Sex Differences in Toddlers' Behavior and Parental Reaction." *Developmental Psychology* 10, no. 4 (1974): 554–58.

Fagot, Beverly, and Richard Hagan. "Aggression in Toddlers: Responses to the Assertive Acts of Boys and Girls." *Sex Roles* 12, nos. 3–4 (1985): 341–51.

———. "Observations of Parent Reactions to Sex-Stereotyped Behaviors: Age and Sex Effects." *Child Development* 62 (1991): 617–28.

Field, T., S. Schanberg, et al. "Tactile/Kinesthetic Stimulation Effects on Preterm Neonates." *Pediatrics* 77, no. 5 (1986): 654–58.

Frisch, Hannah L. "Sex Stereotypes in Adult-Infant Play." *Child Development* 48 (1977): 1671–75.

Gambill, Lionel. "Can More Touching Lead to Less Violence in Our Society?" *Human Touch* 1, no. 3 (1985): 1–3.

Goldbloom, Richard B. "Behavior and Allergy: Myth or Reality?" *Pediatrics in Review* 13, no. 8 (1992): 312–13.

Gordon, Betty Nye. "Maternal Perception of Child Temperament and Observed Mother-Child Interaction." *Child Psychiatry and Human Development* 13, no. 3 (1983): 153–65.

Hall, Wendy A. "New Fatherhood: Myths and Realities." *Public Health Nursing* 11, no. 4 (1994): 219–28.

Haugland, Susan W. "The Effect of Computer Software on Preschool Children's

Developmental Gains." *Journal of Computing in Childhood Education* 3, no. 1 (1992): 15–20.

Jewett, Don L., et al. "A Double-Blind Study of Symptom Provocation to Determine Food Sensitivity." *New England Journal of Medicine* 323, no. 7 (1990): 429–33.

Jordan, Pamela L. "Laboring for Relevance: Expectant and New Fatherhood." *Nursing Research* 39, no. 1 (1990): 11–16.

Jordan, Pamela L., et al. "Breastfeeding and Fathers: Illuminating the Darker Side." *Birth* 19, no. 4 (1990): 210–13.

———. "Supporting the Father When an Infant is Breastfed." *Journal of Human Lactation* 9, no. 1 (1993): 31–34.

Krupper, Jan C., and Ina C. Uzgiris. "Fathers' and Mothers' Speech to Young Infants." *Journal of Psycholinguistic Research* 16, no. 6 (1987): 597–614.

Lamme, Linda, and Athol B. Packer. "Bookreading Behaviors of Infants." *Reading Teacher* 39, no. 6 (1986): 504–9.

Lovestone, S., and R. Kumar. "Postnatal Psychiatric Illness: The Impact of Partners." *British Journal of Psychiatry* 163 (1993): 210–16.

McBride, B. A., and G. Mills. "A Comparison of Mother and Father Involvement with Their Preschool Age Children. *Early Childhood Research Quarterly* 8 (1993): 457–77.

MacDonald, Kevin, and Ross D. Parke. "Parent-Child Physical Play: The Effects of Sex and Age of Children and Parents." *Sex Roles* 15, nos. 7–8 (1986): 367–78.

McKenna, James J., and Sara Mosko. "Evolution and Infant Sleep: An Experimental Study of Infant-Parent Co-Sleeping and Its Implications for SIDS." *ACTA Paediatrica: An International Journal of Paediatrics* 82, supplement 389 (June 1993): 31–35.

Medoff, David, and Charles E. Schaefer. "Children Sharing the Parental Bed: A Review of the Advantages and Disadvantages of Cosleeping." *Psychology: A Journal of Human Behavior* 30, no. 1 (1993): 1–9.

Newman, Philip R., and Barbara Newman. "Parenthood and Adult Development." *Marriage and Family Review* 12, nos. 3–4 (1988): 313–37.

Nicolson, P. "A Brief Report of Women's Expectations of Men's Behaviour in the Transition to Parenthood: Contradictions and Conflicts for Counselling Psychology Practice." *Counselling Psychology Quarterly* 3, no. 4 (1990): 353–61.

Palm, G. "Involved Fatherhood: A Second Chance." *Journal of Men's Studies* 2 (1993): 139–54.

Palm G., and Bill Joyce. "Attachment from a Father's Perspective." *Typescript*, 1994.

Papousek, Mechthild, et al. "Didactic Adjustments in Fathers' and Mothers' Speech to Their 3-Month-Old Infants." *Journal of Psycholinguistic Research* 16, no. 5 (1987): 491–516.

Power, Thomas G., et al. "Compliance and Self-Assertion: Young Children's Responses to Mothers Versus Fathers." *Developmental Psychology* 30, no. 6 (1994): 980–89.

Power, Thomas G., and Ross D. Parke. "Patterns of Early Socialization: Mother- and Father-Infant Interactions in the Home." *International Journal of Behavioral Development* 9 (1986): 331–41.

———. "The Paternal Presence." *Families in Society* 74, no. 1 (1993): 46–50.

Reis, Myrna, and Dolores Gold. "Relationship of Paternal Availability to Problem Solving and Sex-Role Orientation in Young Boys." *Psychological Reports* 40 (1977): 823–29.

Sampson, Hugh A., et al. "Fatal and Near-Fatal Anaphalyctic Reactions to Food in Children and Adolescents." *New England Journal of Medicine* 327, no. 6 (1992): 380–84.

Sorce, James F., et al. "Maternal Emotional Signaling: Its Effect on the Visual Cliff Behavior of 1-Year-Olds." *Developmental Psychology* 21, no. 1 (1985): 195–200.

Stayton, Donelda, et al. "Infant Obedience and Maternal Behavior: The Origins of Socialization Reconsidered." *Child Development* 42 (1971): 1057–69.

Whaley, Kimberlee K. "The Emergence of Social Play in Infancy: A Proposed Developmental Sequence of Infant-Adult Social Play." *Early Childhood Research Quarterly* 5, no. 3 (1990): 347–58.

Whitehurst, G. J., et al. "Accelerating Language Development Through Picture Book Reading." *Developmental Psychology* 24, no. 4 (1988): 552–59.

Resources

Adoption

NATIONAL ADOPTION CENTER offers a great list of questions to ask adoption agencies; addresses tax issues, single-parent issues, and legal issues; provides photos of kids waiting to be adopted, book reviews, lists of state and local contacts, and links to other adoption-related organizations.

1500 Walnut Street, Suite 701
Philadelphia, PA 19102
Tel.: (215) 735-9988
e-mail: nac@adopt.org
http://www.inetcom.net/adopt/nac/nac.html

Advice

FAMILY PLANET has a stable of columnists who dispense advice on just about every topic you can imagine.

http://family.starwave.com/experts/index.html

PARENTSPLACE.COM has one of the largest clearinghouses of parenting advice on the Net.

http://parentsplace.com/

At-Home Dads

"AT-HOME DAD" NEWSLETTER has just about everything a stay-at-home dad could want to know.

Peter Baylies, Publisher
61 Brightwood Ave.
North Andover, MA 01845
Tel.: (508) 685-7931
e-mail: athomedad@aol.com

NATIONAL AT-HOME DADS ASSOCIATION. A resource for all at-home dads who are the primary care providers to their children, this association is designed to help at-home dads connect with one another. NAHDA sponsors a national network for at-home dads and offers an extensive and growing resource list. Contact them for details at:

P.O. Box 1876
Coppell, TX 75019-1876
e-mail: fulltdad@aol.com

or write to Curtis Cooper, founder of the NAHDA, at:
120 Ashbrook Lane
Roswell, GA 30075
Tel.: (770) 643-6964

Babies

FAMILY INTERNET'S BABYCARE CORNER
http://www.familyinternet.com/babycare/babycare.htm

PARENTS' PAGE
http://members.aol.com/AllianceMD/parents.html

Two fact-filled resources written by pediatricians for parents of infants who need basic information fast (treating diaper rash, growth patterns, immunizations, introducing solid foods).

Computers

COMPUTERTOTS
Tel.: (800) 531-5053

Death and Grief

AMERICAN SUDDEN INFANT DEATH SYNDROME (SIDS) INSTITUTE
6065 Roswell Road, Suite 876
Atlanta, GA 30328
Tel.: (800) 232-7437
Fax: (404) 843-0577
e-mail: prevent@sids.org
http://www.sids.org/#Bereavement

SIDS NETWORK
 9 Gonch Farm Road
 Ledyard, CT 06339
 http://sids-network.org/net.htm

Both organizations offer great resources, information, references, and support to help parents and other surviving family members deal with the tragedy of the death of a child.

Divorce

CHILDREN'S RIGHTS COUNCIL has a well-stocked catalog of resources, including a listing of great books on the subject for kids and their parents.
 http://www.vix.com/crc/catalog.htm

SINGLE FATHERS HOMEPAGE
 http://www.pitt.edu/~jsims/singlefa.html

Fun Stuff

BRITE has quite a comprehensive line of parenting aids, child development tools, phonics programs, and teaching ideas.
 http://users.aol.com/clintg777/private/brite.html

CREATIVE CREATIONS has a constantly changing list of twenty fun things to do with kids of all ages.
 http://www.waidsoft.com/funkids.html

ELLEN DAVIS also offers a bunch of fun activities.
 http://ucunix.san.uc.edu/~edavis/kids-list/crafts/easy-and-fun.html

KIDS CRAFTBASE has great suggestions, advice, and products for doing art with kids of all ages.
 http://www.vistek.com/kidcraft.htm

PARENTSPLACE.COM is the parents' resource center on the World Wide Web. It offers a constantly growing collection of articles, advice, and links to other great sites, as well as a newsletter.
 http://www.parentsplace.com

General Fatherhood

FATHER TO FATHER is a wonderful source of information, referrals, and support.

12 McNeal Hall
1985 Buford Avenue
St. Paul, MN 55108
Tel.: (612) 626-1212
http://www.cyfc.umn.edu/FatherNet.htp

FATHERS HOTLINE can refer you to father-friendly organizations in your state or community.

Tel.: (512) 472-DADS (3237)
e-mail: dads@fathers.org

FATHER'S RESOURCE CENTER offers parenting classes, support groups, workshops, legal clinics, and reading lists, and publishes the quarterly newsletter "FatherTimes."

430 Oak Grove Street, Suite 105
Minneapolis, MN 55403
Tel.: (612) 874-1509
e-mail: frc@freenet.msp.mn.us
http://freenet.msp.mn.us/org/frc/index.html

FATHERWORK is a new home page designed to encourage good fathering. The folks at FatherWork view fathering not so much as a social role men play, but as the work they do each day to care for the next generation.

http://fatherwork.byu.edu

NATIONAL CENTER FOR FATHERING has resources designed to help men become more aware of their own fathering style and then work toward improving their skills. Call for a free issue of NCF's quarterly magazine, "Today's Father."

10200 West 75th Street, #267
Shawnee Mission, KS 66204-2223
Tel.: (913) 384-4661
Fax: (913) 384-4665
e-mail: ncf@aol.com
http://www.fathers.com

NATIONAL CENTER ON FATHERS & FAMILIES is a great source of research and data on fathers, father involvement, and so forth.

c/o University of Pennsylvania
3700 Walnut Street, Box 58
Philadelphia, PA 19104-6216
Tel.: (215) 898-5000

NATIONAL FATHERHOOD INITIATIVE offers membership that includes the quarterly newsletter "Fatherhood Today"; updates on family issues and political/legislative developments; the Fatherhood Resource Catalog of books, videos, and audio tapes, offering a discount on all items; and updates on activities and events.

600 Eden Road, Building E
Lancaster, PA 17601
Tel.: (800) 790-DADS or (717) 581-8860
Fax: (717) 581-8862

General Parenting

ERIC CLEARINGHOUSE. More information on parenting than you could ever possibly go through.

Tel.: (800) 583-4135 or (217) 333-1386
e-mail: ericeece@ux1.cso.uiuc.edu
http://ericps.ed.uiuc.edu/ericeece.html

FAMILY PLANET offers links, articles, and resources on just about everything from stranger anxiety to child safety.

http://family.starwave.com/resource/pra/Table_of_Contents.htm

NATIONAL COUNCIL ON FAMILY RELATIONS
Minneapolis, MN
Tel.: (612) 781-9331

"SMART FAMILIES" is a great newsletter published by Family University.
P.O. Box 500050
San Diego, CA 92150-0050
Tel.: (619) 487-7099
Fax: (619) 487-7356
e-mail: FamilyU@aol.com

Health Concerns

NATIONAL ORGANIZATION FOR RARE DISORDERS
    P.O. Box 8923
    New Fairfield, CT 06812-1783
    Tel.: (800) 999-6673

NORTHWEST COALITION FOR ALTERNATIVES TO PESTICIDES (NCAP)
publishes the *Journal of Pesticide Reform* as well as the information packets
"Children and Pesticides" and "Planning for Non-chemical School Ground
Maintenance."
    P.O. Box 1393
    Eugene, OR 97440
    Tel.: (503) 344-5044
    Fax: (503) 344-6923
    e-mail: ncap@igc.apc.org

WEB DOCTOR will answer your specific questions on line.
    http://www.parentsplace.com/readroom/health.html

Music

ADVENTURE KIDS MUSIC AND STORIES
    http://www.rmii.com/dreamweaver/colors.gif

CENTER FOR MUSIC AND YOUNG CHILDREN
    217 Nassau Street
    Princeton, NJ 08542
    Tel.: (609) 924-7801

MUSIC FOR PEOPLE
    David Darling
    Tel.: (203) 672-0275

On-line Conferences, Mailing Lists, and Newsletters

FATHER-L is an e-mail conference dedicated to discussing the importance of
fathers in kids' lives. Send e-mail to listserv@vm1.spcs.umn.edu and write
"subscribe father-l" in the body of the message. If you need more info, send a
message to father-l@tc.umn.edu

PARENTING-L is a great way to get fifty quick, informative answers to just
about any nonemergency question you might have. To subscribe, send e-mail
to listserv@postoffice.cso.usuc.edu with "subscribe parenting-l" in the
subject line.

THE PARENTS' LETTER is published by a pediatrician and filled with good, basic information on such topics as health maintenance, immunizations, illness, behavior, and parenting skills. To subscribe, send e-mail to majordomo@pobox.com with a blank subject line and "subscribe letter" in the body of the message.

OTHER PARENTING LISTS:
  kids-newborn (0–2/3 months)
  kids-infant (3 months–1 year)

To subscribe to one or more of the above, send e-mail to
  listserv@vm.ege.edu.tr using the following format (substituting your own
    name for mine, of course):
  sub kids-newborn Armin Brott
  sub kids-infant Armin Brott

Reading and Other Media
CHILDREN'S LITERATURE provides reviews of the latest kids' books, videos, and computer games.
  7513 Shadywood Road
  Bethesda, MD 20817-9823
  Tel.: (800) 469-2070 or (301) 469-2070 (yes, it's the same number)
  Fax: (301) 469-2071

Temperament
TEMPERAMENT TALK
  1100 K Avenue
  La Grande, OR 97850
  Tel.: (541) 962-8836
  Fax: (541) 963-3572

Toys
VTECH has a wonderful array of high-tech toys for kids six months and older. For a catalog, write or call:
  101 E. Palatine Road
  Wheeling, IL 60090
  Tel.: (800) 521-2010

Travel

FAMILY WORLD HOMEPAGE offers calendars (broken down into four regions) that include information on all sorts of fun places for families to visit in different parts of the country.

http://family.com

Twins

TWINLINE parenting consultation.

http://www.parentsplace.com/readroom/twins/twinline.html

For many more interesting web sites, check out Jean Armour Polly's *Internet Kids Yellow Pages* (Osborne McGraw-Hill, 1996). Despite the title, it's a wonderful source of resources for parents too.

If you have any comments or suggestions about the topics discussed in this book, you can send them to

Armin Brott
P.O. Box 2458
Berkeley, CA 94702
e-mail: armin@pacbell.net

Index

CARTOON CREDITS

About the Author

Armin Brott is a nationally recognized parenting expert and author of *The Expectant Father: Facts, Tips, and Advice for Dads-to-Be*, *The New Father: A Dad's Guide to the Toddler Years*, and *The Single Father: A Dad's Guide to Parenting without a Partner*. He has written on fatherhood for the *New York Times Magazine*, *Newsweek*, the *Washington Post*, *American Baby* magazine, *Parenting* magazine, and many other periodicals. He also hosts "Positive Parenting," a nationally distributed, weekly radio talk show, and lives with his family in Berkeley, California.